5/22

HOSPITALITY SUITE

a play by

ROGER RUEFF

Published by Transcend Press
Chicago, Illinois

ISBN 978-0-9844688-0-5

To all of those who have contacted me over the years seeking this play script. Sorry it took so long.

And to my friends and well-wishers across the globe—many of whose acquaintances I owe to the play itself and our mutual understanding of its issues… and many of whom have produced, directed, and/or performed the play, delighting me in languages I do not speak.

And to Dylan… and my darling Jennifer.

Thank you all.

CHARACTERS

PHIL	A man in his mid-50s.
BOB	A bright young guy who believes what he believes—early 20s.
LARRY	A gregarious man several years younger than PHIL. Energetic, but not manic.
MAN	A man in his middle years.

ACT ONE

Room 2601, the Holiday Inn, Wichita, Kansas. The walls are decorated with innocuous art. The furniture includes: a not-very-stylish sofa; a set of bland, commercial-grade coffee and end tables; matching lamps; and a chair upholstered to match the couch.

Far upstage right or left is a foyer deep enough that the door to the room is not visible. Hidden from view on the other side of the room is the bathroom door, the existence of which is implied by the bathroom light falling on the floor whenever the door is opened. Elsewhere stands glass patio door, with curtains, leading out onto a whitewashed stucco balcony.

Along one wall stands a small wet bar sporting beer, wine, various liquors, sliced lemons, maraschino cherries, and the like—set out in preparation for a party. The wall behind the bar is adorned with a large pastoral picture of indeterminate origin. Nearby is a table or cart with plastic trays upon which lie carrot sticks, celery sticks, crackers, grapes, bowls of dip, and two large cheese balls covered with crushed nuts.

Far downstage left or right is a commercial-grade television set mounted on a swiveling pedestal and facing upstage at a slight angle.

At rise, it is a little after 4:30 p.m., Monday afternoon. The patio door is closed and its curtains have been drawn to one side. The balcony is lit by sunlight entering at a severe angle. The television is on—picture, but no sound. We find BOB *sitting at the one end of the couch with his cell phone to his ear, as if waiting for someone to answer.* PHIL *is sitting at the other end of the couch, leaning forward, attending to paperwork. His briefcase sits open nearby. Throughout much of their conversation,* PHIL *occupies himself with his work.*

PHIL: No answer?

BOB: (*Hanging up*) She must be out shopping.

PHIL: (*Offhand*) God forbid.

BOB: Why do you say that?

PHIL: No reason. It's just something men say when they talk about their wives. One guy says, "She must be out shopping." The other guy says, "God forbid." It's a joke.

BOB: Oh.

(*Beat*)

PHIL: So what do you make of all this, Bob?

BOB: All what.

PHIL: Are you enjoying yourself?

BOB: It sure is tiring.

PHIL: That it is.

BOB: Is this the kind of thing you do all the time?

PHIL: Hell, no. Nobody could stand doing it all the time. You'd go nuts.

BOB: How often do you have to?

PHIL: A few times a year. Sometimes more. Depending.

BOB: I guess that's not so bad.

PHIL: There's a lot to this job. I know it doesn't look like it, but there is.

BOB: I believe you.

PHIL: You have to have people skills. It's not like you can shut yourself away in a laboratory. No offense. You've got to get out there and shake some hands. You can't mind traveling, either. If you have any kind of aversion to traveling, you're in the wrong line of work.

BOB: Do you like to travel?

PHIL: Let's just say I don't mind. It gives me a chance to clear my head.

BOB: I seem to hear a lot of people complain about it.

PHIL: You hear a lot of people complain about a lot of things, Bob, if you listen. The truth is, it's no big deal. O'Hare? Doesn't bother me a bit.

BOB: How come?

PHIL: I just figure, I got a job to do, I'll do it. There's somewhere I need to be, I'll get there. Sooner or later, I'll show up. My worrying won't get me there any faster.

BOB: It seems like most of the people you see in airports, they rush, rush, rush. All the time.

PHIL: Not to get philosophical, Bob, but life requires only as much energy as you decide to put into it.

BOB: What do you mean?

PHIL: You'd be surprised how little effort it takes to live. Some people seem to feel directly responsible for making the sun rise. I'm not one of those.

BOB: You just kinda let things happen, huh.

PHIL: I just don't blow a gasket if they don't always go my way. I mean, so what if the universe doesn't behave exactly the way I want it to. Who am I? Right?

BOB: Right.

PHIL: It also happens to be about the only chance I ever get to read.

BOB: In airports?

PHIL: Airports. Planes. What have you.

BOB: What kind of stuff do you like to read?

PHIL: All sorts of different things. There's almost nothing I won't pick up if it looks interesting.

BOB: You seem to have been at this a long time.

PHIL: To tell you the truth, Bob, I feel like I've been shaking somebody's hand, one way or the other, my entire life.

BOB: You're very good at it.

PHIL: Thank you.

BOB: I mean, judging from what I know.

PHIL: Don't qualify it, Bob.

BOB: Sorry. (*Turning his attention to the television*) I don't think I could handle it.

PHIL: You might be surprised. You did pretty well out there today, from what I could see.

BOB: I like people. I don't mind meeting them.

PHIL: It shows.

BOB: Thanks.

PHIL: Don't close the door too early, Bob.

BOB: I'm not.

PHIL: There's lots of room to move up in marketing, if that's what you're looking for.

BOB: I'm not exactly sure what I want just yet.

PHIL: Just food for thought.

BOB: I know.

PHIL: Not that it really matters to me, anymore. My chances all came and went a long time ago.

BOB: Why do you say that?

PHIL: I'm not complaining. Everybody peaks somewhere. People find their niche. It's nothing to be ashamed of.

BOB: How old are you? If you don't mind my asking.

PHIL: (*Taken aback, but amused*) Geez, Bob. Get a little personal, why don't you.

BOB: Sorry.

PHIL: I'm fifty-six.

BOB: Really?

PHIL: Yeah. Why.

BOB: You don't look it.

PHIL: Thank you, Bob. I will leave you in my will.

BOB: Your secretary said you look distinguished.

PHIL: Oh, really? When was this?

BOB: The other day, when I was talking to her on the phone. I asked her what you look like, so I'd know how to spot you at the airport.

PHIL: And she said I looked distinguished, huh.

BOB: She said your face had character.

PHIL: I will give her the benefit of the doubt and assume she meant that in a favorable vein.

BOB: I'm sure she did.

PHIL: (*Mostly to himself*) I'll have to thank her when I get back. She'll probably make me take her out to lunch.

BOB: (*Thoughtfully*) I wonder sometimes what I'll look like when I get to be your age.

PHIL: Tear my heart out, Bob.

BOB: That's not what I meant.

PHIL: It's okay. I don't mind being fifty-six. I've heard stories of people who lived well into their sixties. I'm only hoping they're true.

BOB: All I mean is that I wonder sometimes how a person attains character. Whether it's something you're born with, that just kind of reveals itself over time. Or whether you have to go through certain things.

PHIL: I couldn't tell you. I don't think about it that much.

BOB: I mean, for all I know, I could be sitting here with a face full of character and just not know it. You think?

PHIL: It's a two-edged sword, Bob.

BOB: I guess.

> (PHIL *wraps a rubber band around a bulging pocket calendar and tosses it into the briefcase, then continues with more work.*)

PHIL: You planning on making a career here, Bob? Doing what you're doing?

BOB: I don't know. I guess that'll depend on whether or not they keep me.

PHIL: How long have you been with the company?

BOB: Six months.

PHIL: Straight out of school?

BOB: Yeah.

PHIL: Well, as a word of advice—which you're free to take or leave—it's never too early to start thinking about where you want to end up. That doesn't mean you have to make a plan. It just means a lot of what happens in the years ahead is going to depend on your priorities. You need to know what they are.

BOB: It's a lot to think about.

PHIL: Yes, it is. But before you know it, somebody'll be handing you a cake with forty candles on it. Maybe fifty. A bunch of people will jump out of a closet and yell "surprise!" Like it's something you haven't been thinking about every waking moment for the past year. You start to wonder.

BOB: It seems like a long way off.

PHIL: But it's not. That's what I'm telling you. Have you got any kids?

BOB: Not yet.

PHIL: Are you planning to? I don't mean to pry.

BOB: Eventually. Sure.

PHIL: That's what'll tell you you're getting old. You see it in your
kids. Or somebody else's kids. One day, the girl next door's eleven,
spindly, looking to babysit. You turn around, she's talking college.
Getting ready to graduate. Making you wish you were eighteen.
That's what makes you feel old. When you realize they attract you
as members of the opposite sex, and still, in your mind, you
remember when they were six. It makes you feel like a pervert.

BOB: Do you have kids?

PHIL: Four of 'em. All girls.

BOB: You're kidding.

PHIL: I was always a singles hitter in high school. Never could hit the
home run.

BOB: I take it you wanted a boy.

PHIL: As long as I was going to go to the trouble to have four kids, it
would've been nice. Yes. (*After a moment*) The night my youngest
was born, I went out into the hall and cried.

BOB: Because she was a girl?

PHIL: Not that I'd ever tell her.

BOB: Sure.

PHIL: What time do you have?

BOB: (*Checking his watch*) Twenty to five.

PHIL: I wonder what's keeping Larry.

BOB: Do you not carry a watch?

PHIL: No. I do not.

BOB: How come?

PHIL: The world is full of clocks, Bob. I found that out. Clocks and
mirrors. It's some kind of conspiracy.

> (PHIL *finishes his paperwork with a flourish and tosses it
> into the briefcase.* HE *pulls out a magazine, then closes the
> briefcase and sets it aside.*)

BOB: (*Distantly, staring at the television*) I'd like a boy someday.

PHIL: (*Settling in for some recreational reading*) Maybe you'll get lucky.

(*Beat*)

BOB: What's that you're reading?

PHIL: (*Showing the magazine*) Penthouse.

BOB: (*As if he has committed an indiscretion*) Oh.

PHIL: You're welcome to it when I'm done.

BOB: That's okay.

PHIL: You don't want it?

BOB: No. Thanks. (*Something he feels compelled to add by way of explanation*) I don't look at magazines like that.

PHIL: You don't?

BOB: No.

PHIL: Are you one of those who believes that magazines like this should not be published?

BOB: I'm one of those who believes they shouldn't be purchased.

PHIL: (*Quietly amused*) That's a clever answer.

BOB: I wasn't trying to be clever.

PHIL: I know. But you were, anyway. You stated your distaste for this kind of thing without actually attacking the First Amendment. That takes talent.

BOB: I just said what I thought.

PHIL: That's what I mean. You did it without thinking. That's what makes me think you may have a career in marketing.

BOB: What does your wife have to say about you reading magazines like that?

PHIL: It's not my wife's concern, Bob.

BOB: It's not?

PHIL: We're divorced.

BOB: Oh. Sorry.

PHIL: It's okay.

BOB: How long had you been married?

PHIL: Long enough to have four girls.

BOB: (*Cautiously, after a moment*) Do you mind if I ask you what the problem was?

PHIL: (*After a moment, without offense*) Maybe you should try your wife again.

BOB: Sorry.

PHIL: It's all right.

> (BOB *takes out his phone and dials.*)

BOB: It's just that I have a real hard time imagining what it must be like to be divorced.

PHIL: The picture becomes crystal clear in a very short period of time. Believe me.

BOB: I hope I never have to find out.

PHIL: I hope you don't, either.

BOB: (*Hanging up*) Went straight to the answering machine.

PHIL: At least she's not out shopping, anymore.

BOB: Huh? (*Smiling politely, as it dawns on him*) Oh, yeah.

PHIL: Divorce is never pretty, Bob. I wouldn't wish it on anybody.

BOB: Jesus said if a man divorces his wife, he causes her to commit adultery.

PHIL: I am aware of what Jesus said concerning divorce.

BOB: You are?

PHIL: You're not the only one who's ever gone to church.

BOB: I didn't mean that. (*A little eagerly*) What church do you go to?

PHIL: I was speaking in the past tense.

BOB: You mean you don't go, anymore?

PHIL: No. I don't.

BOB: How come?

PHIL: Because I no longer believe in Jesus. There was a time I did, but I don't, anymore.

BOB: Why? Did something happen?

PHIL: No. It was just a decision I made as a young man that I felt pull away from me over time. It was like shedding a skin.

BOB: I've always been taught that when a person is saved, Jesus seals him for all eternity.

PHIL: So was I, Bob.

BOB: But you're saying that isn't true?

PHIL: Listen, Bob. Do you mind if we change the subject?

BOB: How come?

PHIL: Because I feel something inside of me turning you off, and I don't want that to happen. My instincts tell me you're a bright young guy, and you've probably got some interesting things to say.

BOB: I do. But a lot of them center around Jesus.

PHIL: Okay. But those are the ones I don't want to hear. So find the others, all right? Search yourself for those items of interest that have nothing to do with Jesus.

BOB: (*After a moment of deliberation*) I can't think of any, offhand.

PHIL: Well, then let's be silent for a while. Maybe they'll come to you.

> (*Pause.* BOB *dials again.*)

BOB: I didn't mean to offend.

PHIL: You didn't, Bob. Don't worry.

> (BOB *gets through and begins to converse quietly with his wife.* LARRY *enters and stops abruptly, as if dumbstruck.*)

LARRY: (*Shocked disbelief*) This is it?

PHIL: (*Matter-of-factly*) Hello, Larry.

LARRY: This is fucking IT?

PHIL: What do you mean, "is this it?" Of course this is it. What did you expect?

LARRY: Phil. Buddy. The operative word is "suite", my friend. Hospitality *suite*, not hospitality *closet*. There's no room in here.

PHIL: It's the best I could do on short notice.

LARRY: Where do you expect people to stand? Out in the hall?

PHIL: What're you bitching about? It's on the twenty-sixth floor, for Christ's sake. Look at the view.

LARRY: Phil! We're in Wichita, Kansas, man! What does it matter whether we're on the first floor or the five-hundredth floor? It all looks the same.

PHIL: Well, next time, you can make the arrangements.

LARRY: (*Grumbling, as* HE *crosses to the patio door*) Murdock would've had a room four times this size.

PHIL: Yeah? Well, Murdock isn't here, is he.

LARRY: (*Looking out onto the balcony*) You can say that again. Well, at least we have something to jump off of when nobody shows.

PHIL: Fuck you, Larry.

LARRY: (*Mock indignation*) Terrific. That's what I get for having aesthetic values. Foul language thrown in my face.

PHIL: Do you know Bob? From the research center?

LARRY: (*Cordially*) Sure. We've met. How ya doin', Bob?

> (BOB *signals hello.*)

PHIL: He's on the phone to his wife.

LARRY: Well, far be it from me to interrupt a man in the throes of matrimonial discourse. (*Taking in the room*) I only hope his wife does most the talking. We gotta conserve what little oxygen we have.

> (LARRY *spies the array of foodstuffs on the table.*)

LARRY: What is this?

PHIL: What does it look like.

LARRY: You tell me.

PHIL: It's hors d'oeuvres.

LARRY: (*Flabbergasted*) You call these hors d'oeuvres?

PHIL: Don't start with me. All right?

LARRY: Phil! These are not hors d'oeuvres, my friend. This is— I don't know what this is. Sliced carrots, celery sticks, ranch dressing and a couple of overgrown cheese balls?

PHIL: This entire thing was spur of the moment. You know that.

LARRY: Do you know what that tool-and-die outfit downstairs is serving? Do you have any idea what they're eating on the twenty-fifth floor?

PHIL: I don't know, and I don't want to know.

LARRY: Shrimp, my friend. Jumbo shrimp. On ice. Oysters on the halfshell. All kinda weird French cheeses. These little puff pastry things. That's hors d'oeuvres, Phil, my friend of many years. Not this. Downstairs, they wouldn't let a celery stick near the place. They'd make you check it at the door.

PHIL: Well, then go spend the night downstairs.

LARRY: I just might have to. Jesus Christ. (*To* BOB, *who has just ended his call*) Do you believe this, Bob?

BOB: Looks okay to me.

LARRY: That's exactly my point. You don't know anything. No offense. But how many of these things have you been to?

BOB: Just one.

LARRY: This one. Right?

BOB: Yeah.

LARRY: Precisely. Well, who knows, Phil; maybe we'll get lucky, and everybody who walks in here tonight will be a first-timer, like Bob.

BOB: Is there some kind of problem?

PHIL: No, Bob. There is no problem.

>   (LARRY *goes to the bar and fixes himself a drink.*)

LARRY: So how ya doin', Bob? We didn't really get a chance to say hello before.

BOB: I was on the phone with my wife.

LARRY: I know. You were talking about furniture. Right?

BOB: (*Startled*) How did you know?

LARRY: Bob. You don't stay married to the same woman for sixteen years and not know when somebody's talking to his wife about furniture. She's found something. Right?

BOB: Well.

LARRY: Am I right?

BOB: She thinks she has.

LARRY: It's the same thing, Bob. That's like saying a shark thinks it smells blood in the water. A moth thinks it sees a light bulb. She's zeroing in.

BOB: She was just asking what I thought.

LARRY: And what did you tell her?

BOB: I told her—

LARRY: (*Interrupting*) You told her you'd like to see it. Right? You said it sounded very nice, but you're not sure you can afford it right now. You'll have to see.

BOB: How did you know that?

LARRY: It's what we all tell our wives, Bob. It's what every man since Adam has told his wife when she said she's found a piece of furniture. It's instinct. Salmon swim upstream to spawn. Birds fly south in the winter. Once every four years, lemmings throw themselves off a cliff. And we, as husbands, tell our wives we're not sure we can afford it right now when they talk about buying furniture.

BOB: Then how come so much furniture gets bought?

LARRY: I didn't say they listen. Hell, no. That's not the point. The point is that it gets said. We know perfectly well we're gonna come home one day and find whatever it is sitting in the living room. Then we get mad, there's a fight, things are said. One thing leads to another, and eventually the two parties wind up in bed. It's Nature's way, Bob. The purpose of Nature is to get people into bed. Mostly in pairs.

BOB: (*Amused*) Is that right.

LARRY: Absolutely. That's why, if you go there on your own, voluntarily, you can save yourself a whole heap of trouble. (*To* PHIL) Speaking of the purpose of Nature. Did you happen to catch some of the stuff walking around the floor today?

PHIL: You mean the women?

LARRY: Unless you've changed preference since the last time we talked, Phil. Yes, I mean the women.

PHIL: How could you tell what they looked like? They were all wearing business suits.

LARRY: That's exactly what I mean. They were all wearing business suits. Exactly.

PHIL: (*Unamused*) Oh, that's right. You like 'em in business suits, don't you.

LARRY: You bet your life I do. There's something about a woman in a business suit that drives me wild. It's like they're all tied up in a neat little package—just waiting for somebody to come and tug on the one little cord that sets everything free. A woman in a business suit is my idea of art. (*Struck with an important corollary*) Jean skirts, too. I don't know why, but I've always been a sucker for a jean skirt. Maybe there's some connection, Bob. Whaddya think?

BOB: I'm sure I couldn't tell you.

LARRY: I must've fallen in love a hundred times today.

BOB: Are you sure it was love?

LARRY: It felt like love. All the symptoms.

BOB: How can you fall in love with a hundred different women in one afternoon?

LARRY: I don't know. It's one of those wonderful mysteries of life. Maybe that's what I kept fallin' in love with. Life, itself. Maybe I was just happy to be part of a world populated by creatures who look like that. I had the overwhelming desire to thank each and every one. Personally.

  (BOB *suppresses a chuckle.*)

LARRY: So tell me, Bob. What kind of woman's attire gets your motor running?

BOB: I don't know.

LARRY: No favorites, huh.

BOB: I try not to think about it.

LARRY: You try not?

BOB: I'm married.

LARRY: Well, yeah, Bob. I see the ring. I'm just asking what direction your tastes run.

BOB: (*Uncomfortable with the question*) I don't know.

LARRY: Oh. (*Studying* BOB) Bob. Lemme ask you something. Seriously.

BOB: What.

LARRY: Are you gay?

PHIL: Larry!

LARRY: No, I'm just saying. He seems to be lacking one of the fundamental traits of the American male. Which I could understand if you were, you know. But you're not. At least I think you're not; you're married.

BOB: I just don't see any reason to let my eyes go wandering all over God's creation, when he's given me a very wonderful woman to be my wife.

LARRY: Oh, I see. So you're a spiritual man, huh.

BOB: That's part of it.

LARRY: They blind you when you get saved, do they?

BOB: Jesus said if you look on a woman with lust, it's the same as committing adultery.

LARRY: Well, I think there's a fair number of wives in this country who might disagree, Bob. No offense. It just seems to me there's a line gets crossed somewhere.

BOB: In fact, he said that if your eye causes you to sin, you should gouge it out and cast it away from you.

LARRY: He did, huh. Well, he must never have seen a woman in a business suit. If he had, who knows—we might have a whole different kinda religion. One where lusting is a sacrament.

(LARRY *grabs a carrot stick from the vegetable tray.*)

PHIL: Hey. I thought you weren't interested in my hors d'oeuvres.

LARRY: I'm just tasting, Phil; I'm not actually partaking. I'm making sure nobody's gonna gag.

PHIL: Well, don't eat the whole thing up.

LARRY: (*To* BOB, *as* HE *continues to pick at the tray*) You know why you're here, dontcha, Bob?

BOB: Not really. No.

LARRY: You mean, nobody told you?

BOB: Nope. All they said was get on a plane and be here.

LARRY: Jesus Christ. No wonder this company's never gotten off the runway. You're here for cosmetic purposes, Bob. For what you represent.

BOB: What do you mean?

LARRY: You're here to represent Research. Technical support. The brains of the company, as it were.

BOB: Me?

LARRY: Absolutely.

BOB: But I don't have that much experience.

LARRY: It doesn't matter, Bob. You as a person are not really here. It's what you represent.

BOB: Am I supposed to do anything?

LARRY: Nope. Just stand there and look wise. Or sit. It's up to you.

PHIL: You'll do fine, Bob.

BOB: (*A little awed*) Geez. I hope so.

LARRY: If you wanna know the truth, Bob, nobody is really here. You think you see people walking around up and down the halls?

You don't. What you see is functions. That's the nature of a convention.

BOB: Functions?

LARRY: That's right.

PHIL: What Larry means, Bob, is that there's a certain detachment that takes place at these things. If you look at it from the standpoint of why we're here, what we are is more important than who we are. So, in a certain sense, we're just... functions.

BOB: That's seems kind of impersonal.

LARRY: Of course it's impersonal, Bob. Why do you think they hold conventions at places like this? Is there anything about this place that smacks of personality to you? Of course not. It's a utility shelf. A place to rest the functions overnight. If they held conventions at places that had a human feeling about 'em, probably nothing would get done.

BOB: It seems a shame.

PHIL: It's not a shame, Bob.

LARRY: That's right. It's just the way things are.

BOB: Still.

LARRY: Everybody represents something, Bob. You take us, for example. Me and Phil. Now I, as a salesman, represent the lips of the company. Blowing kisses. Making our product line—i.e., industrial lubricants of all manners and types—look appealing to those who might be in the market. My job, in a nutshell, is to seduce. Phil, on the other hand, as account manager, represents the company's prick. Consummating the deals that I have helped to set up. And, dare I say, you won't find a bigger prick in the industry. Isn't that right, Phil.

PHIL: Blow it out your ass, Larry.

LARRY: That brings up an important point, Bob. Foul language and rude gestures are essential to any kinda success in marketing.

BOB: If I started using foul language, my wife would throw me out of the house.

LARRY: That's all the more reason. Right, Phil?

>   (PHIL *shoots* LARRY *a warning glance.* LARRY *quickly
>   redirects.*)

LARRY: So who do they have you working for these days, Bob?

BOB: Dr. Young.

LARRY: Jim Young?

BOB: Yeah. Why? You know him?

LARRY: We've met.

BOB: Tremendous guy.

LARRY: Oh yeah? How so.

BOB: What do you mean?

LARRY: In what way is he tremendous?

BOB: (*As if it should be obvious*) I don't know. He's got what... twenty or thirty patents? He's involved in all sorts of professional societies. I think he's even a deacon in his church.

LARRY: And all this makes him tremendous, huh.

BOB: Well. The patents alone.

LARRY: Are they his patents, Bob?

BOB: What do you mean?

LARRY: On all these various patents. Is his the only name that appears at the top? Or are there others.

BOB: I don't know. I've never actually seen one. Why do you ask?

LARRY: There are people, Bob, who stick their names on patents, even though they had nothing to do with the idea.

BOB: I'm sure he would never.

LARRY: There are people, Bob. That's all I'm saying.

BOB: Who put their names on somebody else's patent?

LARRY: You bet your life. There are people who work themselves into positions of authority so that they can weasel their way onto patents they had nothing to do with.

BOB: Yeah, but I can't believe—

LARRY: I'm not accusing, Bob. I'm just saying. There are people.

BOB: Well, I guess that's why there's such a thing as professionalism.

LARRY: Do you want to know about professionalism, Bob? Do you want me to tell you? There are no professionals, Bob. In the whole wide world there are none. There are people who do things and other people who don't do those same things. That's all.

BOB: (*Mystified*) So you don't consider Dr. Young a professional?

LARRY: Look, Bob. No offense. I know you admire the man and all. But I'll tell you something about Jim Young.

BOB: What's that.

LARRY: He's an idiot.

BOB: What!

LARRY: He's a moron, Bob. I wouldn't trust the guy to wax my car.

BOB: How can you possibly say that?

LARRY: I've met him. Remember? I've gotten an earful of Jim Young on more than one occasion, and I can tell you for a fact he's full of shit.

BOB: Well, I don't think so. And I work with him every day.

LARRY: Then maybe you don't know what to look for.

BOB: I guess not. (*Diplomatically*) Or maybe I just have different standards.

> (LARRY *is arrested by the comment.* HE *studies* BOB *for a moment.*)

LARRY: Lemme tell ya something, Bob. You got a minute?

BOB: Sure.

LARRY: There are people in this world. Lots of them. Who, if given half a chance. Are you listening?

BOB: Yes.

LARRY: There are people who, if you let them, put on a serious face to do business. Who try to look very official when they're doing what they're doing. And do you know why?

BOB: Why.

LARRY: Because they don't know what they're doing. Because, if you know what you're doing, you don't have to look like you know what you're doing. It happens naturally. You follow me?

BOB: Sure.

LARRY: But it's the people who don't know what they're doing who put on this serious look all the time to try to make you think they do. And you know how you tell the difference?

BOB: No.

LARRY: You don't know?

BOB: No. I mean, I don't think—

LARRY: That's okay. Because you're young, and you've got time to learn. But here's how you tell. The way you tell is, if you hear a little voice. And the voice says to you, "This guy who is sitting before me, he is lying through his teeth and feeding me bullshit." Or "she," because this is not the world of our fathers, and thank god for that; it wasn't fair. Am I right?

BOB: Sure.

LARRY: So this guy or this woman is spewing manure and smiling so you won't catch on—only you know it anyway, because of the voice. What do you do.

BOB: What do you mean?

LARRY: What do you do.

BOB: You mean if I'm sitting there?

LARRY: Yes. If you're sitting there being dumped on. What do you do.

BOB: I don't know.

LARRY: Exactly.

BOB: What?

LARRY: You hit it right on the nose. And you know why?

BOB: I don't even know what I just said.

LARRY: Because for you and nearly every other person in this world, that voice is way off in the distance. You're not even sure you hear it. You do, but you're not sure. Which is why the world's in the state it's in. Because if people listened to those voices, we would all be better off. The voices are there to help us survive, but we—and I'm speaking on behalf of the entire human race now, the whole species—we don't listen. We stuff our ears with cotton so that we don't hear. And for a very simple reason: Because it costs too much. Because to listen to those voices, you gotta put things away.

BOB: Put things away?

LARRY: Sure. You say to yourself all the time, Bob—whether you realize it or not, "There's things I want in this life. Y'know? A nice car. A home somewhere. Kids. Whatever. And if I listen to those voices, something bad will happen to me. I will set myself apart from others. I'll lose my job. I will lose something of what I am." You follow me?

BOB: I think so.

LARRY: Good. You're on track. Only you're lying to yourself, see?

BOB: What do you mean?

LARRY: You're lying to yourself. You're saying, on the one hand, "If I lose my job, or whatever, I will not be able to fulfill the various desires that I have," when, in reality, your true desire is to shut this motherfucker up. See? It's fear. It's the fear of not having what you think you want. That's why you sit there and eat horseshit from this son-of-a-bitch who's smiling at you through his teeth. Now, do you follow me?

BOB: Sure. It's a kind of fear.

LARRY: Exactly. Only it's not a "kind of" fear, Bob. It is fear. It's the fear of death that plugs our ears, because it doesn't want us to hear it coming. Because if we could hear it, we would avoid it. We would step out of its way.

BOB: Out of the way of death?

LARRY: Out of the way of the fear of death, Bob. The fear. No, hell. Nobody steps out of the way of death. It's too big. There's nowhere to step.

BOB: Jesus said death can be conquered.

LARRY: We're not talking religion here, Bob. There's a time and a place for that. This is two guys talking, so don't go getting religious on me, okay? It interrupts the flow of things.

BOB: I'm just telling you what he said.

LARRY: I am aware of that, Bob. But this is not that. This is something else.

BOB: Still. It's what I believe.

LARRY: Good for you, Bob. I'm glad that you believe. It's a fine thing to believe. But what I'm telling you is that it's irrelevant. I believe that the sun will rise in the east tomorrow morning. I would wager a goodly portion of my salary. But I'm not about to bring it up at this juncture because it's irrelevant. Do you see what I'm saying?

BOB: Sure, but—

LARRY: Okay. So no religion. Because I'm making a point here.

BOB: Which is what?

LARRY: Which is, as I'm sure you're curious to find out, what would I do.

BOB: What do you mean?

LARRY: What would I do. You're sitting there in the background at another table with seven billion of your peers, watching me have lunch with this guy, and he starts feeding me what he's talking about with this serious look on his face, which has thrown up all my warning signs. What do you suppose I'd do.

BOB: I don't know. Confront him?

LARRY: "Confront" him? Bob? Here's what I would say to him. I would say, "Buddy? I have heard a lotta horseshit in my time because, God knows, I'm a salesman, and we all have to wade through our share of snow to get to the cabin. But you take the cake. I don't believe you have the first idea what you're talking about. Your children admire you, I'm sure—as we all hope they do. And maybe your wife doesn't know. But I know. And my knowledge forces me to call you on the fact that you're a goddamn cocksucking liar from the word go." And then I would sit down and finish my soup.

BOB: You would not.

LARRY: (*Defending his pride*) Phil. Have you or have you not ever heard or seen me do what we were just talking about?

PHIL: (*Not looking up from the magazine*) Yes.

LARRY: There. You see? That's why there's hope, Bob. Because there's people like me who listen.

BOB: (*To* PHIL) When was this?

LARRY: Whaddya mean, "when"? Are you doubting the word of a man who sits there reading Penthouse to expand his mind? Are you going to question that?

PHIL: It was a couple of years ago. At lunch with a purchasing agent.

LARRY: You see?

BOB: You actually said that?

LARRY: (*Proudly*) Word for word.

PHIL: It was not word for word.

LARRY: In principle, Phil. I'm speaking to the boy in principle, because, after all, he's a bright young man and he understands the meaning of a concept. (*To* BOB) Am I right?

BOB: (*Off-balance*) Sure.

LARRY: Therefore, in a global sense—in a universal sense—in principle. Yes. I said that. Word for word. In principle.

BOB: So what happened?

LARRY: What do you think happened? What would you expect to happen?

BOB: The guy got mad?

LARRY: The guy was furious. He sat there through the rest of the meal, not saying a word, like there was a fire burning somewhere inside him that nobody was supposed to know about. And not another drop of doo-doo spilled from his lips the whole time.

BOB: He didn't do anything?

LARRY: What could he do? He was called. Everybody acknowledged what an ass he'd been all along. Nobody said anything, but it was out in the open. They knew.

BOB: Did you lose the account?

LARRY: Of course, we lost the account. You can't speak to a man like that and expect to keep the account. And if you do. If you say that to a man, and he puts down his fork and says to you, "Bob. You are absolutely right. I have been faking like I know what I'm talking about from the moment I sat down, and I'm sorry. Not to you, because I don't owe you anything. But to myself, because I want to be the best human being I can possibly be, and I want to be honest above all else." Then you forget about the account, Bob. You forget about everything. You shave your head and put on a saffron robe, and you sell pictures of this guy at the airport. Because he has no fear and he just proved it. He deserves to be worshipped.

BOB: (*A little shell-shocked*) Wow.

LARRY: "Wow" is right, Bob. "Wow" sums it up quite nicely.

BOB: I can't believe you actually did that.

LARRY: Somebody had to. It just fell to me because I listen.

BOB: Yeah. But to say that.

LARRY: Do yourself a favor, Bob. All right?

BOB: What.

LARRY: Don't ever become one of those people.

BOB: You mean… what we were just talking about?

LARRY: Yes. Don't ever become one. Right?

BOB: I wouldn't. At least I hope not.

LARRY: Don't promise me, Bob. A promise to me means nothing. Just keep yourself from that. I don't want to have to confront you at lunch someday like I did that other guy. But I will, for your own sake, because I like you. So just avoid that, is all I'm saying. Okay?

BOB: Sure.

LARRY: Good. Now. Can I get you something to drink?

BOB: No. I have to excuse myself.

LARRY: I can fix you something while you're on the throne.

BOB: No thanks. I just need to go.

    (BOB *exits into the bathroom.*)

PHIL: Who wound you up?

LARRY: Nobody wound me up. I'm just excited. That's all. I've got a good feeling about tonight. We're gonna do some business.

PHIL: You're sure about that, are you.

LARRY: Absolutely. There's business in the air. Smell it? That's the fragrance of contacts being made. Deals being worked out. The kind that makes account ledgers grow.

PHIL: There's only one that matters to us this trip.

LARRY: I know. But we're gonna get that one, too, man. You just watch. Fuller's gonna come walking through that door. Take one look around. He will be so stunned, so overwhelmed with the fact he's on the twenty-sixth floor, overlooking all of Wichita, Kansas, like some ancient king surveying his fiefdom. Larry predicts. He will throw himself onto the carpet, prostrate at our feet. And he will say, "You talk to me about moxy. Anybody with the aesthetic wherewithal to pick this, of all places, for a hospitality suite must certainly have the right line of industrial lubricants for my application. As a matter of fact, it strikes me you guys probably have everybody's right lubricant, only they can't see it, because their eyes haven't been opened like mine have by the light from above."

PHIL: He's going to say all that, is he.

LARRY: Word for word. And y'know what I'm gonna tell him? I'm gonna say, "Mr. Fuller. You're absolutely right. We do have the right line of lubricants for your application. Especially your plant in Gary. And I, personally, would be proud to handle the account. But there is one thing that I ask of you as a favor. To help us get better acquainted."

PHIL: Which is?

LARRY: "That you take me as your concubine. Or Phil, if you think he's better looking." I figure we offer him a package deal. I'll do the cooking and the laundry. You do the bathrooms. We'll take turns keeping him happy in bed.

PHIL: You really think he's gonna go for us, huh.

LARRY: He has to, Phil. You name me one other supplier out there on the floor today who can give him the same thing we can. Who's got both the technology and the follow-up. I'm telling ya, there isn't one. If he's got any kinda decent head on his shoulders, he will ignore the tainted advice of his inferiors and get us in for at least a trial run.

PHIL: And what if he doesn't.

LARRY: If he doesn't go for us?

PHIL: Yeah.

LARRY: Well, then I think what we do is: We pack our bags tomorrow morning. Catch the breakfast flight home. Wander into the office about half past two. And then hang ourselves in the bathroom by our ties.

PHIL: I wish to hell we'd had more than three days notice.

LARRY: Well, you know the business world. There's two kinds of companies; the quick and the dead. An opportunity sneaks up and taps you on the shoulder, you throw it on the bed and make love to it. In the morning, you find out its name.

PHIL: Do you even know what this guy looks like?

LARRY: No. Couldn't find a thing online. You?

PHIL: Unh-unh.

LARRY: What about Bob?

PHIL: How would Bob know?

LARRY: Yeah. Well. It doesn't matter, anyway, thank God. That's the one nice thing about conventions. All God's chillen wear nametags. Especially the first night out. And especially a guy like that. You think he won't wear his nametag? He probably had one made special. Neon. With little flashing lights. "Dick Fuller: President—Frontier Manufacturing. The man you've never seen and only heard about. Nickname: El Kahuna Grande." Can you imagine the treatment that guy's gonna get? Everywhere he goes.

"Can I get you another shrimp to go with that champagne, Mr. Fuller? You have such a rapier wit, Mr. Fuller. Are you in the market for a 'yes' man?" I only hope he's wearing a ring I can kiss.

PHIL: You sound like you're in love with the guy.

LARRY: I can't help it, man. I get a hard-on just thinking about size of that account. Do you realize what it would mean if we managed to get one plant? Just one? Even Gary? We're talking sell-out. We would have to farm stuff out just to keep up. Okay, so the margins drop a little. Who cares. Volume's up. We're making money hand over fist in Gary. And for the first time in years, this company is up on its feet and running with the big boys. No more of this same old same old following us around, like an albatross. And y'know what else? It'll serve those sons-of-bitches in Manufacturing right for giving us shit all these years about how we're not selling anything. How they got all these little shit accounts they can't keep track of. And personally, Phil—not to rub it in or anything—but I'm gonna say, "Fuck you guys. I've had my troubles, and now you've got yours. You've been sitting on your asses for so long now, you've forgotten how to make anything." And Evans is gonna send us to England to have us knighted.

PHIL: I'll believe it when I see it.

LARRY: (*Suspicious*) You sound like you know something.

PHIL: I don't.

LARRY: You put in the call. Right?

PHIL: Right.

LARRY: And he's coming?

PHIL: As far as I know.

LARRY: Well, then what's to worry about? We've got technology alien civilizations only dream about. Both of us know how to grovel. (*Indicating the bathroom*) And, to top it all off, we've got window dressing from the research center to stand there and make us look smart. I'm telling you, it's in the bag.

PHIL: I hope you're right.

LARRY: (*Genuinely concerned*) Is he okay?

PHIL: He hasn't been feeling very well.

LARRY: How come?

PHIL: I don't know. Maybe he caught something.

LARRY: What's there to catch? Nothing's going around.

PHIL: Well, then, maybe it's nerves. Maybe he just wasn't ready for the likes of you. Especially when you give it to him with both barrels like that.

LARRY: Me? Naw, I'm just talking to him.

PHIL: I don't think he sees it that way.

LARRY: The boy's gotta learn. There's other things in life besides what he thinks he knows.

PHIL: He's a nice kid.

LARRY: Sure he's a nice kid. I wouldn't waste my time with him, if he wasn't. That's the last thing I need is to groom another asshole for the lubricants industry. Lord knows, we've got our share already. But he counts too much on his niceness. I want to give him a fallback position.

PHIL: He's got his religion.

LARRY: After that. I want him to know it's not the apocalypse, if he stumbles. That there's life and meaning in the world, apart from that. (*Thoughtfully*) Besides. He reminds me of you in a lot of ways.

PHIL: No, he doesn't. He reminds you of yourself.

LARRY: Yeah, but I take after you, so it all works out. (*Considering the bathroom*) Or who knows; maybe he's just basking in the experience.

PHIL: Of going to the bathroom?

LARRY: Sure. Have you been in there yet?

PHIL: No. Why.

LARRY: It's terrific, man. It's the only thing I like about this place. They got spotlights over the johns. Makes you feel like a star. That, and they got mirrors on three sides, so you can watch yourself wiping your ass.

PHIL: That a major goal of yours, is it?

LARRY: I think it's something everybody should experience at least once in their lifetime. Do you realize what the ancient kings of Egypt would've given to be able to watch themselves wiping their own asses? Plenty. But they couldn't, because the technology was unavailable.

PHIL: They had mirrors.

LARRY: Hand mirrors, Phil. Little bitty jobs. It's not the same thing. You watch yourself wiping your ass in a hand mirror—you can't even tell what's going on. You might as well be watching somebody else. To do it right, you need full-fledged wall-to-wall mirrors. Then you get the total picture. It reminds you you're not all that much different from anybody else, when it comes down to it. Gives you a sense of humility.

PHIL: If you say so.

(LARRY *inadvertently glances at the television.*)

LARRY: (*Urgently*) I'll be a son-of-a-bitch. Phil! C'mere quick.

(PHIL *joins him and looks at the screen.*)

PHIL: What is it.

LARRY: (*Pointing at the screen*) Tell me this guy doesn't look like an alien being.

PHIL: (*Annoyed*) Get outta here.

LARRY: That doesn't strike you as strange? That there's a guy walking around who looks like he's from another world?

(BOB *emerges from the bathroom.*)

LARRY: Hey, Bob. C'mere a second.

BOB: (*Joining him*) What.

LARRY: (*Indicating the screen*) Tell me what you think this guy looks like.

BOB: Which guy?

LARRY: That guy right there. First impression.

BOB: (*After a moment, innocently*) I don't know. Phil, maybe?

LARRY: (*As if struck with a startling revelation*) Y'know, you're right? Phil, buddy. What's the deal here, man? Is there something we should know about you?

BOB: What's he talking about?

PHIL: Ignore him, Bob.

LARRY: That's right, Bob. Ignore me. Pay no attention to the greatest mind of this or any century. You'll find out.

BOB: (*Amused*) You're crazy.

LARRY: (*Innocent pride*) That's what they said about Charlie Manson.

PHIL: Are you all right, Bob?

BOB: Yeah. Fine. I'm just a little queasy is all.

LARRY: You need something? We can call down.

BOB: No, thanks. I just need to relax a minute.

LARRY: Did Phil have you on the floor all day?

BOB: Some of it.

LARRY: Working the booth?

BOB: Yeah.

LARRY: Well, no wonder. You should've told him to go fuck himself. I don't blame you; I hate working a booth. I only do it if I absolutely have to. And even then, only if I can't get out of it.

BOB: I thought it was kind of interesting.

LARRY: Anything's interesting for a while, Bob. Dental surgery is interesting for a while. But certain things get old in a hurry. Isn't that right, Phil.

PHIL: It's something that has to be done.

LARRY: There you are, Bob. Words handed down from on high. "It's something that has to be done." Just like life.

> (PHIL *searches through his last pack of cigarettes and finds it empty.*)

PHIL: Can I bum a cigarette off you, Larry?

LARRY: You could ordinarily, Phil, my friend. But not anymore. I gave it up.

PHIL: You did not.

LARRY: Swear to God.

PHIL: When?

LARRY: Coupla months ago. You would, too, if you knew what was good for you.

PHIL: Fuck you, Larry. You're not my wife.

LARRY: You're absolutely right, Phil; I'm not your wife. And it's good of you to point that out. Because, as close as we are, I sometimes forget.

PHIL: I wonder if that place downstairs is still open.

BOB: It should be. I thought I saw a sign that said they stay open until six-thirty.

LARRY: Bob, here, has got more sense than the two of us put together. He's never smoked a cigarette in his life. Have you, Bob.

BOB: No, I haven't.

LARRY: I thought so. You got that look about ya. I bet you don't drink much, either.

BOB: An occasional beer, now and then.

LARRY: But nothing hard, right?

BOB: No.

LARRY: And correct me, if I'm wrong. But I'm willing to bet—I would even lay money. That never in your life have you walked into a strip joint, jumped up onstage, grabbed the dancer, taken her down on the ground, and fucked her brains out. Right there in front of everybody.

BOB: (*Shocked*) I never what?!

PHIL: Jesus, Larry!

LARRY: Just answer the question. Yes or no.

BOB: No! Geez! I've never even been near a place like that!

LARRY: See? That's what I'm saying, Bob. You oughta apply for sainthood. Competition's not as stiff as it used to be. I think you stand a good chance of getting in. You Catholic?

BOB: No.

LARRY: Episcopalian?

BOB: No.

LARRY: What, then.

BOB: Baptist.

LARRY: Oh. Well, that is a problem. (*Puzzling over the issue*) They must have something like that, though. For people who go their whole lives without doing anything?

BOB: Not as far as I know.

LARRY: (*With great conviction*) Well, then, dammit Bob; it's time to change religions. Go somewhere you're appreciated—where there's a chance to move up. You let me know if it happens, too. Right?

BOB: You'll be the first.

LARRY: Remember. It was my idea. I get dibs on the concession. Little plastic statues and things like that.

(PHIL *dons his suit coat and heads for the door.*)

LARRY: (*To* PHIL) Where are you headed?

PHIL: I'm going to run downstairs and see if that place is still open. I'll be back in a few minutes.

BOB: I'll go with you.

PHIL: No. You stay here. Somebody has to keep an eye on Larry. Make sure he doesn't sublet the place.

LARRY: Hey. While you're down there, check out the twenty-fifth floor. See what it looks like when people know what they're doing. That is, if you can live with the shame.

(PHIL *exits.*)

LARRY: (*Calling after*) And bring me back some shrimp! (*Privately, smiling*) What a nut.

BOB: Him or you?

LARRY: Him. The guy cracks me up.

BOB: He's not the one I'd exactly call a nut around here.

LARRY: That's because you don't know him. You want a carrot stick, Bob?

BOB: How long have you two worked together?

LARRY: That depends on what you mean. You want a carrot stick?

BOB: No. Thank you.

LARRY: (*Partaking of the hors d'oeuvres*) In the sense of geologic time, we just met. In dog years, on the other hand, we go way back.

BOB: What about in human years?

LARRY: Human years? We've known each other "a while", I guess. Why do you ask?

BOB: He strikes me as an interesting guy.

LARRY: (*Sincerely*) That's one helluva man, Bob, lemme tell ya. You're looking for somebody to admire; pick Phil. Not that asshole, Jim Young.

BOB: How long has he been divorced?

LARRY: I don't think he is, officially. I believe it's still pending. But I'm not sure about that, so don't quote me.

BOB: You think there's any chance of he and his wife getting back together?

LARRY: God, I hope not.

BOB: Why do you say that?

LARRY: Because his wife, Joanne, is an industrial-strength bitch. With strong genes, apparently, because his daughters are bitches, too. All except the oldest one, who's learning you can't treat people that way and get away with it.

BOB: You know his whole family?

LARRY: Sure. We used to chum around together. Not so much anymore, but there was a time. My wife and his still keep up.

BOB: I think it's a shame that he has to get divorced.

LARRY: He doesn't have to, Bob. Nobody's putting a gun to his head. It's a choice he's making. To gain something else.

BOB: Like what?

LARRY: I don't know. His freedom, I guess.

BOB: It still seems like an awful lot to give up.

LARRY: Sometimes you gotta chew off your leg, Bob, to get out of life's traps.

BOB: I guess.

LARRY: How long've you been married?

BOB: Six months.

LARRY: Do you love your wife?

BOB: Of course. Why wouldn't I?

LARRY: I don't know. People get married for a lot of different reasons. You seem like a very principled guy to me.

BOB: So?

LARRY: So, I've known people. I'm not saying you're one of 'em, Bob—just that I've known them. Who were real principled. And then they met somebody else who was real principled, and the two of 'em got married. Only to find out, one day, that it was their principles that got married. That the two of them just kinda came along for the ride.

BOB: Oh.

LARRY: Love has a lotta counterfeits, Bob. Not to get deep.

BOB: Sure.

LARRY: Phil's gone through a lotta changes in the last few years. And I don't just mean the divorce.

BOB: Really? How so?

LARRY: He used to be the real manic-depressive type. One day, he'd be riding in the clouds. The world was a beautiful place, and he was just happy to be here. The next day, you wouldn't even know you were talking to the same person. He'd walk around looking like somebody'd let the air out of him. You got the impression that, at any moment, he might pull out a gun and shoot himself. Even then, he was real personable. It just seemed like something inside of him had kinda collapsed. I mean, and who can blame him, with his living situation. Right?

BOB: What do you mean?

LARRY: Well, let's face it, Bob. He was living in a house with five women. The youngest of which was just past puberty; the oldest of whom had not yet gone through menopause. Y'know what that means, dontcha. Five times a month, somebody was on the rag. That's almost continuous, Bob. That's the kinda thing Dante wrote about. Did you ever read "The Inferno"?

BOB: No.

LARRY: Well, do sometime. You'll find out at the very bottom of Hell, they've got Satan up to his ying-yang, buried in a sheet of ice. And, below that, there's a room where they lock you up with five women, each of whom is still having her period.

BOB: I don't remember reading anything like that in the Bible.

LARRY: Of course not. It's too horrible. Who would print it. But I tell ya one thing. If I saw a stained glass image of a scene like that, I'd repent in a second.

BOB: (*Seriously*) So Phil was manic-depressive, huh.

LARRY: I don't know the clinical definition, Bob. That was just my impression. The important thing is that he's found some way to center himself. I don't know what it is, and frankly I don't care. As long as it works.

BOB: The things you don't know about a person.

LARRY: That's why God gave us eyes and ears, Bob. To find out. Except for some things, which are none of our goddamn business.

BOB: Sure.

LARRY: (*A cautionary note*) Look. Bob. Ask me whatever you want about Phil. Okay? I'll be happy to tell you, if I think you're being sincere. But don't ask him directly. All right? The man's been through a lot. He doesn't need to be pressed.

(PHIL *enters, smoking a cigarette.*)

LARRY: Speak of the devil. Where's my shrimp?

PHIL: Fuck you. Eat a carrot, if you're so goddamn hungry. Have some cheese.

LARRY: I don't want cheese. I want shrimp.

PHIL: Well, then call room service. Have them send something up.

LARRY: I would, but I don't wanna embarrass you in front of the boy.

PHIL: Believe me, Larry. As long as I've known you, nothing you could possibly do or say would embarrass or surprise me in the least.

LARRY: (*Going to the bar*) See what I put up with, Bob? Twelve years now. But one of these days, no more. I'll come into work with an Uzi, and you'll read about us in the newspapers the next day. You sure I can't get you something to drink?

BOB: Maybe just a Coke.

LARRY: Coming right up. What's yours Phil? Black Russian? Vodka martini with a twist?

PHIL: Club soda.

LARRY: Club soda?

PHIL: That's right. Club soda. With a lime.

LARRY: You feeling all right?

PHIL: I gave up drinking.

LARRY: You did? When?

PHIL: A while back.

LARRY: (*Fixing the drinks*) Well, I'll be a son-of-a-bitch. I don't smoke, you don't drink, and Bob, here, wouldn't think about lusting after a woman. Between the three of us, we're practically Jesus. Which reminds me. Who's gonna bartend tonight.

PHIL: I figured Bob would.

BOB: Me?

PHIL: Do you mind?

BOB: Well, like I said, I'm not really accustomed to drinking hard liquor.

PHIL: Nobody's asking you to drink it, Bob. We're asking you to serve it.

BOB: Still. I won't know what I'm doing.

LARRY: (*Demonstrating*) There's nothing to it, Bob. Look. You pour stuff into a glass. See? Now you know bartending.

BOB: What about the formulas?

PHIL: They're called "recipes," Bob. And that's no problem, either. We'll call down and get you a book.

BOB: But what if somebody wants something exotic?

LARRY: Perfect. The only reason people order exotic drinks is to show how sophisticated they are. If they have to tell you how to make it, so much the better. It makes 'em feel like experts.

> (LARRY *crosses to* PHIL *and* BOB *with the drinks in hand.*)

PHIL: Larry and I are gonna have our hands full, Bob.

BOB: Well. I'll try.

LARRY: That's all we ask, Bob, is that you try.

BOB: (*Taking his drink*) Thank you.

> (LARRY *gestures for a toast.*)

LARRY: Gentlemen. To the profound religious experience that comes from doing a good job and being underpaid.

PHIL: Happy days.

> (THEY *drink.*)

LARRY: (*With satisfaction*) Thank you, Jesus.

BOB: Amen.

LARRY: (*Checking his watch*) So, what time's this thing supposed to start, anyway.

PHIL: Seven.

LARRY: You guys hungry?

BOB: I am. A little.

LARRY: Phil?

PHIL: I could probably eat something, I guess.

LARRY: What're you in the mood for?

BOB: I saw a place down the street that advertises "home cooking."

LARRY: God, no. The way my wife cooks? That's the last thing I want.

PHIL: Maybe we just better head downstairs.

LARRY: Sounds like a good plan to me. We fill our bellies with hotel food, ogle the waitresses a little...

(PHIL *shoots* LARRY *a mildly disciplining glance.*)

LARRY: Or not. (*Encouragingly*) Then we come back here and show Bob the ropes. Teach him what it's like to do business.

BOB: I'm looking forward to it.

LARRY: So. You think you're ready for this big stuff, Bob?

BOB: (*Bravely*) Well, I guess there's only one way to find out. And that's to throw me in the water and see if I can swim.

(LARRY *casts* PHIL *a knowing look, then turns to* BOB.)

LARRY: I think you're missing the point here, Bob. We're about to throw you off a cliff and see if you can fly.

(BOB*'s bravery collapses into apprehension. Lights fade quickly to black.*)

ACT TWO

SCENE ONE

Around midnight that same evening. The room is strewn with five hours worth of party debris (dirty glasses, crumpled napkins, and the like). The cheese balls are but shadows of their former selves, and most of the other food has disappeared. The patio door is slightly open—for ventilation. The television remains on with picture but no sound. BOB *stands behind the bar, sipping a soft drink.* PHIL *is trying to usher the last guest from the room.* HE *is quite congenial in doing so, especially considering that the* MAN *is in pretty much of a drunken stupor.*

MAN: (*Summarily, extending his hand*) Well, sir. I wanna thank you for a delightful evening. And for the liquor.

PHIL: Don't thank me. Thank my friend here. He's the bartender.

    (BOB *smiles uneasily.*)

MAN: And a damn fine one, at that. I have never in my life seen anyone put that much hootch in a screwdriver.

BOB: (*A bit off balance*) Thanks.

MAN: You musta done this kinda thing for a living at one time or another.

BOB: Well... no.

MAN: I tell you what, by God. You most certainly could. That's for damn sure. (*Chummily*) If you ever get tired of workin' for this old fart—

BOB: Oh, I don't work for...

    (PHIL *gives* BOB *a high sign telling him it's not worth answering.*)

MAN: If you ever get fed up, just keep in mind there's a career for ya somewhere, tendin' bar. Believe me, son. You got the gift.

BOB: Thanks.

MAN: Ya just never know, either. A man needs somethin' to fall back on, now and again. (*To* PHIL) Isn't that right.

PHIL: You bet.

BOB: Are you staying in the hotel?

MAN: (*Puzzled*) I beg your pardon?

BOB: I just wondered if you might need a ride somewhere.

MAN: A ride?

PHIL: Bob, here, was just concerned for your safety. In case you had to head out on the road.

MAN: (*To* PHIL, *with conviction*) And don't think I don't appreciate it. Goddammit, I mean that. A lotta young kids these days, they could care less. They figure, a man gets killed in the street. He's layin' there. It's just one less rung to hafta climb. You know what I'm sayin'?

PHIL: Sure.

MAN: (*To* BOB) Don't ever lose that, son. You're okay.

PHIL: Are you sure you're going to be all right?

MAN: Oh, hell yes. I'm right downstairs here somewhere. If I can just locate my key. Don't you worry none. I'll find my way home.

PHIL: Well, take care now.

MAN: You bet I will. (*To* PHIL, *reiterating an important tip*) And as a final word of advice; I'd think long and hard about my loyalties, if I were you. I am tellin' you that this is the year of the Boilermaker. They have got the talent. They have got the coaching. Which way's the elevator?

PHIL: Down there on the right.

MAN: There's a championship in the works. You mark my words.

PHIL: (*Politely*) Time will tell.

> (PHIL *ushers the* MAN *into the hall and returns momentarily, in a huff.*)

PHIL: (*In disgust*) They've also got the easiest fucking schedule on planet Earth. Hell, my old high school team could beat anybody in the Big Ten. Jesus Christ.

BOB: (*Amused*) What a character.

PHIL: That son-of-a-bitch sat here talking basketball to me for nearly two hours, Bob. And all he did was make it clear he doesn't know the first thing about the game. That's what kills me about these things. You get a guy away from his wife for a couple of days, pour a few drinks into him, and suddenly he's the world's foremost expert on sports. That's why God created wives, Bob. To let men know when they're being assholes. You get a man away from his wife for any length of time, and he doesn't have the first idea how he's behaving.

BOB: The Bible says God created Eve as a helpmeet.

PHIL: A what?

BOB: A helper for Adam, suitable to meet his needs.

PHIL: Well, I don't know about that. As far as I'm concerned, God created women to be mirrors. So a man could see himself. See what an ass he is. You talk to me about souls, Bob. I'm telling you, a man doesn't have any idea what his soul looks like until he gazes into the eyes of the woman he's married to. Then, if he's any kind of decent human being, he spends the next few days throwing up. An honest man can't stand the sight.

BOB: I thought you didn't like being married.

PHIL: I didn't. That doesn't mean I don't recommend it. There's lots of things in this world that are good for you that aren't necessarily pleasant. Like circumcision.

> (LARRY *enters—still energetic, but looking a little time-worn.*)

PHIL: Well, it's about time. Where the hell've you been?

LARRY: Whaddya mean, "where've I been." Where do you think I've been. For the last two hours, while you've been sitting here stroking every swinging dick that walked through that door, I've been out in search of the Grand Kahuna.

BOB: The what?

LARRY: The Saviour, Bob. El Presidente. The man who, with one small utterance—one tiny ejaculation of sound—could make this company big with child.

PHIL: Did you find him?

LARRY: Phil. Use your intuition here for a second. Employ your God-given gift for smelling out the truth of a situation. Do I look as though I found him?

PHIL: No.

LARRY: Good. You still got it.

BOB: Who are you guys talking about?

LARRY: We are talking, Bob, about The Grand Kahuna. The Great White Whale. Did you ever read "The Old Man and the Sea"?

BOB: No.

LARRY: Well, then forget that. What we're talking about is a man who represents, as an entity, the largest single account this company has, or probably will have, ever seen.

PHIL: Potential account.

LARRY: Potential. Yes. And it's good of you to point that out, my friend. What could have been. Because it was our job—yours and mine—to turn that potentiality into reality. To have it show up in the coffers. To court this gentleman. To promise him favors, if necessary. To get him on our side. (*To* BOB) To render meaning, Bob, to the lives of those who exist for no other reason than to manufacture industrial lubricants bearing our beloved trademark. (*To* PHIL) But did we succeed in that regard, or did we fail? Let's see a show of hands.

   (LARRY *raises his hand high in the air.*)

PHIL: We'll be all right.

LARRY: Of course, we'll be all right. Once they drag our bodies from the river and send our spirits to the moon. Sure, then. It's all the intermediate stuff, Phil. It's the actual process of being skinned alive and set fire to. That's the difficult part. The rest is duck soup.

PHIL: Have a drink and sit down. There's nothing we can do about it now.

LARRY: (*Grumbling, on his way to the bar*) Have a drink, he says. Whaddya think I've been doing for the last five hours. Sucking back cocktails and making small talk.

BOB: You had to go searching for this guy? How come?

LARRY: We weren't supposed to, Bob. We had to, yes. But no, we weren't supposed to. He was supposed to show up here tonight. According to "the plan." (*Pointedly, for* PHIL*'s benefit*) Somebody was supposed to have called him and confirmed an invitation. Someone was supposed to have lured him up here for a drink. Someone was supposed to have done that.

PHIL: What're you looking at me for? I did my job.

LARRY: You're sure you called him?

PHIL: You're damn right I called him.

LARRY: And you spoke to him direct.

PHIL: I spoke to his secretary. He was on the phone long distance. She assured me he would be here.

LARRY: Yeah? Well, she was kidding. She probably had a bunch of her secretary friends all gathered around a speaker phone, saying, "Watch this." I bet she does stand-up on the side.

PHIL: Something probably just happened.

LARRY: Sure, something happened. I think it's rather obvious that something happened. My guess is, he walked through that door, took one look at what passes for hors d'oeuvres up here, and ran for his life. Ignoring completely the fact that he was on the twenty-sixth floor, overlooking all of Wichita, Kansas. "Something happened." That's rich.

BOB: Maybe he pulled up sick at the last minute.

LARRY: Oh, he's here all right. I heard his name being bandied about, all night long. In the present tense. He's here, my friends. He just isn't here, if you catch my subtle nuance. (*To* PHIL) Therefore, you and I. Collectively. Are fucked.

PHIL: We are not fucked.

LARRY: Okay, "screwed" then. Shat upon. However you want to say it. Reamed. In deep doo-doo.

PHIL: We'll just have to find another way. That's all.

LARRY: Phil. Are you deaf? I'm sitting here telling you we lost the man. He was invited, but he did not come. We spilled our seed upon rocky soil, whereupon it did not grow, and neither did we reap. We're like the dinosaurs when the climate changed; there is no longer any reason for us to roam the Earth. We are, in a word, fucked.

BOB: Can't you just schedule an appointment to go see him?

LARRY: You don't schedule appointments with this guy, Bob. He's the president. He refers you to his people.

BOB: So why not get in touch with one of his people?

LARRY: Because they're a bunch of dildoes. Every one of 'em. There are people in this world, Bob, in positions of authority who shouldn't be. Who get in bed with somebody. A certain supplier, let's say. And who refuse to get out, no matter what. You come at them with something demonstrably superior to what they're using, and y'know what they say to you? They say, "Fuck you, buddy. We are not in the mood to try anything new." Completely discounting the fact that they're losing money hand over fist because of all the equipment failures and whatnot that you could prevent, if they would let you. Nobody wants to change things, Bob. That's why. Sometimes. You have to go past the smaller minds. You have to cozy up to someone a little higher on the ladder, who can say to them, "I would like you very much to consider what this new product might mean to our operation. Meditate on it. Get in touch with your true feelings. Then either buy some and give it a try, or get the fuck out, because you're fired." And that, in a nutshell, is what Phil and I were here to do. (*To* PHIL) But which we did not do, Phil, my friend. Ergo. Q-E-D. We are fucked. The both of us.

PHIL: I'll call his secretary tomorrow.

LARRY: Phil! Are you not hearing anything I'm saying? It's human nature, I realize, to believe that we stand another chance with this guy, but it's fantasy, man. Here's a couple others that may shock you, too. One, there is no Santa Claus. And two, y'know that money you used to find when you'd leave a tooth under your pillow? Your dad put it there. I'm sorry to tear down your entire philosophical framework, my friend, but it's time to face facts. We're gonna go back to Chicago, and Evans is going to say to us, "Phil? Larry? Come on into my office for a second. I've got something for you. Bend over."

(LARRY *collapses into a chair.*)

LARRY: So whaddya think, Bob. You wanna do this for a living?

BOB: I don't know. I thought it was kinda interesting.

LARRY: Oh, yeah? How so.

BOB: You hear lots of interesting stories.

LARRY: That you do. They are far outweighed by the horseshit that flies across the room all night, but they're there if you listen for them, I guess.

BOB: Are there always this many people?

LARRY: It just seemed like a lot of people, Bob. Because the room's so damn small.

PHIL: (*Exasperated*) Larry!

LARRY: Sorry, Phil. The carrot sticks have gone to my head.

BOB: I got ahold of some guy who started talking to me about dogs.

LARRY: About dogs?

BOB: Yeah.

LARRY: What about dogs.

BOB: Just that he's always owned one. He told me that, one way or the other, he's owned a dog his entire life. Most of them German Shepherds.

LARRY: Lotsa people own dogs, Bob. It's not that unusual.

BOB: I know. But it got us talking about all sorts of other things. It turns out he just had to have one put to sleep, because it bit somebody. So then he started telling me about the one he owned before that and the one before that. And before you knew it, we had traced his entire life through this series of dogs. Some really fascinating stories.

LARRY: (*Despondently, staring at the television*) I wish to hell Murdock were here.

BOB: Who's Murdock?

LARRY: Dale Murdock. Best damn marketing rep this company has ever known. Jesus, what a talent.

BOB: Successful?

LARRY: More than just successful, Bob. He had "the gift." Y'know how some athletes? You watch 'em at what they're doing, and it looks like something they're remembering, instead of something they had to learn? That's how it was with Murdock—only with people. There was a time—somebody told me this story; I don't know if it's true—Murdock was at one of these things, pitching tires. And there was a guy sitting over in the corner all by himself. People come alone to these things, sometimes. It happens. Anyway, Murdock sees this guy sitting there and feels sorry for him. So he takes one of the tires and rolls it across the room to where the guy's sitting. Then he looks at him and says, "Whaddya think?" Of course, the guy doesn't know what to think. Somebody just rolled him a tire. So what. So Murdock says,... "Imagine the ride." See what I mean? That's the kinda stuff he was good at. Making people feel at ease. It was a subtle little piece of genius. He didn't make a big deal out of it; he just did it.

BOB: Who was the guy?

LARRY: It doesn't matter, Bob. The guy's not important to the story. Except that, suddenly, he felt like he was part of things. Poor bastard didn't know anybody, and now, all of a sudden, he's paid attention to. Did they ever do business? Who knows. But I guarantee ya one thing. Never in his life did that guy forget the name of Dale Murdock. He probably framed his card and hung it on the wall.

BOB: Where is he now?

LARRY: Who? Murdock?

BOB: Yeah.

LARRY: He's gone to his great reward.

BOB: Oh.

LARRY: He's down in Florida, somewhere, I think.

PHIL: Last I heard, somebody told me he owns a chain of Burger Kings.

LARRY: I wouldn't doubt that for a second. Probably the biggest damn chain in the state. (*With resignation*) But the days of Murdock are behind us, my friend. These are the days of Larry and Phil. Phil and Larry. However you wanna say it. Two guys who are about to be royally fucked up the ass.

PHIL: We'll be all right.

LARRY: You think so, huh.

PHIL: Sure.

LARRY: Well, I hope you're right, for both our sakes. Because letting Mr. Fuller slip through our fingers like this could be construed by some as an act of incompetence. It makes us look pretty bad.

BOB: Did you say Fuller?

LARRY: Yeah.

BOB: Dick Fuller?

LARRY: (*Despairingly*) Yeah. Dick. Why? You know him?

BOB: That's who I was talking to.

LARRY: Whaddya mean?

BOB: The guy with the dogs. That was Dick Fuller.

LARRY: Get outta here.

BOB: I'm serious. Look. He even gave me his card.

> (BOB *digs a business card from his pocket and hands it to* PHIL.)

PHIL: (*Reading*) Well, I'll be a son of a bitch.

LARRY: (*Grabbing the card*) Lemme see that.

PHIL: I thought you said you checked everybody's nametags.

LARRY: I did, Phil. Swear to God. And anybody who wasn't wearing a nametag, I came right out and asked them, "What is your name?" That's why I don't see how there's any way—

BOB: He wasn't wearing his nametag.

LARRY: What?

BOB: I mean he wasn't wearing his own. It was somebody else's.

PHIL: Why on Earth would he be wearing somebody else's nametag, Bob?

BOB: Beats me. It looked like he'd had a couple of drinks before he got here. Maybe he swapped with somebody. I got the impression he wanted to be left alone. He was awful broken up about the dog.

LARRY: I do not fucking believe this! Dick Fuller. Right within our grasp, and we missed him, Phil. We had our fingers on the man, and we let him slip away.

BOB: Sorry.

PHIL: It's not your fault, Bob.

LARRY: Right here, Phil. He was ours.

PHIL: Next time, you better ask people for their names, whether they're wearing badges or not.

LARRY: I got news for you, my friend. For us, there will be no "next time." We had Dick Fuller within our sphere of influence, and we allowed him to leave without hearing a thing from us of what we had to say.

PHIL: We'll be all right.

LARRY: What all did you talk about, Bob?

BOB: I don't know. Stuff.

LARRY: What kind of "stuff"?

BOB: Just... different things.

LARRY: Can you be a little more specific? I mean, did you talk about the weather? Sports? What.

BOB: Dogs, mostly.

LARRY: That's all?

BOB: Well, that and stuff about our families. He asked about my wife.

LARRY: Your wife?

BOB: Yeah.

LARRY: What did he wanna know about your wife, Bob?

BOB: Nothing. He just asked.

LARRY: Did you tell him he could have her if he wanted? In consideration for throwing a little business our way?

PHIL: Larry!

LARRY: What else, Bob. What other things did you talk about.

BOB: Just... I don't know. Religion... some.

LARRY: (*Dumbfounded*) Religion?

BOB: Yeah.

LARRY: You talked to the president of one of the largest manufacturing firms in the Midwest about religion?

BOB: Is that what he is? I didn't know.

LARRY: What did you tell him, Bob? What exactly did you say to him about religion?

BOB: We just talked.

LARRY: I know that. What I'm trying to find out is, what did you say? You didn't contradict him, did you.

BOB: No.

LARRY: Thank God. That's the first rule of talking religion at one of these things, Bob. Don't contradict anyone. Especially a customer. I take that back. It's the second rule. The first rule about talking religion at a convention is, don't.

BOB: Don't what?

LARRY: Don't do it. There's plenty of other things to talk about without getting into that. And the second rule is, whatever you do, don't contradict a client. Potential or otherwise.

BOB: What if you think they're wrong?

LARRY: They're not wrong, Bob. That's the third rule. If they're in a position to do business with you, and they have a good credit rating, then for a brief time anyway, they have the corner on absolute truth. Theirs is the copyright. Understand?

BOB: What if a couple of them get to talking, and it turns out they disagree?

LARRY: Then you back away, Bob. You find yourself somewhere to hide. You take cover and watch for flying glass.

BOB: You mean you don't think it's possible for people to have a civil conversation about religion?

LARRY: No, Bob, I don't. Except in certain rare circumstances. Within the confines of a church sanctuary, for instance? Where everybody's supposed to be on their best behavior? Fine. There? No problem. In a church basement? Well, that's iffy. I've seen some knock-down-drag-out fights break out in a Sunday School class. But here, Bob. At a convention. Absolutely not. That's why there's the first rule.

BOB: We seem to have survived.

LARRY: Did you contradict him?

BOB: No.

LARRY: That's why, Bob. That's the reason you survived.

BOB: I thought it was a real nice chat.

LARRY: How the hell did you end up talking religion, anyway?

BOB: It came up. With the stories of his dogs dying and all.

LARRY: Did you tell him his dogs were in heaven?

BOB: No.

LARRY: You told him they were in hell?!

BOB: Of course not.

LARRY: What then, Bob? What on Earth did you say to him?

BOB: We just started talking. The thing about the dogs was just a lead-in. It started us talking about life and death.

LARRY: (*Carefully, after a moment*) It was a "lead-in," Bob?

BOB: That's right.

LARRY: Which implies, does it not, that you were looking for the opportunity to speak to someone about life and death.

BOB: I guess so. Sure.

LARRY: It's not "sure," Bob. Don't say "sure" to me like I'm supposed to know. Because people in general do not go around looking for opportunities to strike up conversations about life and death. Religion and things of that ilk.

BOB: Some people do.

LARRY: Some people, Bob. Yes. There are people. And, apparently, you're one of them. But most people, no. It's not something that comes up. Most people, if you bring up the subject, will say that life is good and death is bad. The end. They do not go around looking for chances.

BOB: Well, then I guess I'm just not most people.

LARRY: That you are not, Bob. I think that's very safe to say.

BOB: I just think it's important to let people know what you believe.

LARRY: Jesus Christ.

BOB: If I had known it was somebody you were supposed to get in touch with, I would have told you. I would've alerted you, somehow.

PHIL: It's not your fault, Bob.

LARRY: Phil!

PHIL: It's not. How could he have known? He was just talking.

LARRY: Talking. Yes. Granted. But listening? No. I don't think so. At least not for opportunities to advance the interests of the company. If the conversation had stayed on a more temporal plane, then perhaps, just maybe, it would've worked itself around to the point that something about lubricants would have been mentioned.

PHIL: You don't know that.

LARRY: I think the odds would've been a helluva lot better. As it was, however, the conversation was not allowed to follow a natural course. Somebody was at the helm, directing it. Am I right? Bob?

PHIL: It sounds like the guy just wanted to be left alone.

LARRY: That's not the point, and you know it.

BOB: Phil's right. He practically came out and said it.

LARRY: (Exasperated) But it was our job, guys. Compadres. To overcome that desire of his, at least for a little while. To garner his interest. And as far as that goes, if he was really that intent on being left alone, he would've stayed in his room, wouldn't he. He wouldn't have gone out cruising the hospitality suites. I submit to you, my friends, that he did not, in fact, desire to be left alone, but only not to talk business.

PHIL: In which case, we're out of luck anyway.

LARRY: No, Phil. Because there's ways of getting around that, and you know it. Not to badger the man. But to let him know what we came here to tell him. That's what I'm saying.

BOB: I'm sorry.

LARRY: It's too late for you to be sorry, Bob. It doesn't do us any good.

BOB: What else can I do?

LARRY: Nothing. There is absolutely nothing you can do, Bob. Now. At this juncture. (*After a moment, strategizing*) Did he happen to mention where he was staying?

BOB: Somewhere in the hotel.

LARRY: This hotel?

PHIL: Larry, what are you going to do. Go pounding on his door? It's after midnight.

LARRY: I'm just asking. All right? Is there a crime in that? Because I'm wondering if maybe tomorrow, at breakfast, we could accidentally run into him in the coffee shop. Accidentally.

PHIL: We don't even know what he looks like.

LARRY: Bob does.

BOB: I'd be willing to do that. Sure.

LARRY: Just outta curiosity, Bob. What was he wearing?

BOB: A sport shirt, I think. And jeans, if I'm not mistaken.

LARRY: Jeans?

BOB: Or some other kinda casual pants.

LARRY: Jesus. No wonder I didn't think to ask him his name. He didn't look like anybody.

PHIL: (*Examining the back side of the card*) What's all this business on the back of the card, Bob?

BOB: That's where he said he was going after he left here.

LARRY: What!

BOB: It's some kind of private party at that hotel down the street.

(LARRY *snatches the card.*)

LARRY: Well, why didn't you say so, Bob! What the hell are we standing around here for! Let's go!

BOB: We can't.

LARRY: Whaddya mean, we can't.

BOB: It's supposed to be by invitation only.

LARRY: So?

BOB: So, I think he'd get mad, if we all showed up like that. He made a real big point of saying how private it was.

LARRY: That's the least of our worries, Bob. If he gets mad, we'll work our way around it. Grab your coat.

PHIL: Not so fast, Larry.

LARRY: Now what.

PHIL: Bob may be right. I'm not so sure it's a good idea to go barging in on this guy.

LARRY: Phil!

PHIL: Think about it. Do you really want to piss this guy off by crashing some kind of exclusive party? Not to mention who else might be there.

LARRY: Well, what do you propose we do? Stand around here in a circle jerk while the account of a lifetime slips away?

PHIL: No.

LARRY: What, then.

PHIL: I think we send Bob.

LARRY: (*Quietly, flabbergasted*) What?

PHIL: He gave you this as an invitation. Didn't he, Bob.

BOB: He told me it would get me in.

LARRY: (*Painfully*) Phil-Phil-Phil-Phil-Phil. Don't do this to me, man!

PHIL: What choice do we have? It's our only legitimate way of being there. Besides… (*Trying to mask his own apprehension*)… he knows Bob. They've talked. Bob's got an in.

LARRY: You're putting our future in the hands of a kid, Phil. (*To* BOB) No offense, Bob. I like you. I'm sure if we lived next door to each other, we'd get together for barbecues, but you just don't have a lot of experience with things like this.

PHIL: He'll be fine, Larry. Give me your card.

LARRY: (*Mumbling, as* HE *digs into his pocket for a business card*) Jesus Christ.

> (PHIL *takes* LARRY*'s card, then pulls out one of his own and writes on the back.*)

PHIL: Here's what you do, Bob. Are you listening?

BOB: Yes.

PHIL: I want you to go down the street and see if you can find Mr. Fuller. If you are fortunate, and he's still there, I want you to hand him our business cards and tell him that we're very anxious to meet with him as soon as is humanly possible. You got that? Tell him we'll be around all morning tomorrow, and that we are at his beck and call. He can reach us at either of these numbers. Ask him would he please get in touch with either Larry or me, so that we can talk to him—very briefly—about business. Explain that we know he's busy; we won't keep him long. There are just a few things we'd like to discuss. Can you do that?

BOB: Sure. I'll try.

PHIL: That's all you have to do, Bob. Just hand him the cards and get out.

BOB: What if he wants to talk?

LARRY: Well, then you go ahead and talk to him, Bob. Forty days and forty nights, if you have to. Until he tires of it, comprenday? And then you come back and tell us what happened.

BOB: You'll wait up?

LARRY: Until the next fiscal quarter, if we have to. Beyond that, I can't say.

PHIL: You'll do fine, Bob. Don't worry.

LARRY: That's right, Bob. I'm sorry for doubting you. You'll do fine. If you follow those instructions to the letter. Understand?

BOB: Yes.

LARRY: Good. Now, go. Time's a wasting.

BOB: Okay. See you guys later.

> (BOB *exits quickly.*)

LARRY: (*Calling after*) And hurry! But not too fast! You work up a sweat, he won't come near you! So take your time! But hurry!

(*Pause*)

LARRY: Do I strike you as a religious man, Phil?

PHIL: Not in the slightest.

LARRY: Then why am I suddenly possessed by the overwhelming desire to pray.

(*Blackout*)

SCENE TWO

A little after 1:00 a.m. The room is dimly lit. LARRY *sits staring blankly at the television, to which there is still no sound.* PHIL *stands at the patio door, staring out into the night, smoking a cigarette. Much of the ensuing conversation (especially on* PHIL's *part) carries with it a general tone of detachment.* LARRY *rarely take his eyes from the television as* THEY *speak.*

PHIL: What time is it.

LARRY: (*Indignant*) Whaddya mean, "What time is it." Why don't you buy yourself a watch, for God's sake. Then you won't have to always be asking people what time it is.

    (*Beat*)

LARRY: I've got a good mind not to tell you. Just to let you sit there, wallowing in your ignorance. Wondering what time it could possibly be. Not knowing. (*After a moment, checking his watch*) It's ten after one.

PHIL: Thanks.

LARRY: I wonder if he found him.

PHIL: He found him.

LARRY: What makes you so sure?

PHIL: If he hadn't've found him, he'd be back by now.

LARRY: Not necessarily. He might be down on the street corner, preaching to a wino.

PHIL: He's all right.

LARRY: (*Tiredly*) Yeah.

    (*Beat*)

LARRY: Phil, lemme ask you something. Seriously.

PHIL: What.

LARRY: Are you on any kind of medication I should know about?

PHIL: What do you mean?

LARRY: Not that it's any of my business. I'd just like to know. For curiosity's sake.

PHIL: What makes you think I'm taking medication?

LARRY: Because I've never seen you this relaxed before. I almost get the impression that you just don't frankly give a shit.

PHIL: I don't.

LARRY: No. I mean, I know that. We all don't give a shit to a certain extent. What I'm saying is, it's like you don't care.

PHIL: I'm tired, Larry.

LARRY: I recognize that, Phil. It's been a very long day.

PHIL: That's not what I mean.

LARRY: (*Cautiously, after a moment*) I know what you're driving at, and I sympathize. Really, I do. We all know you've been going through a lot, lately. And for a long time now, I've been meaning to state outright that if there's anything you need. At all. I'm serious. Day or night. You don't hesitate to give me a call. I would've said something before, but I thought maybe it was understood.

PHIL: I assumed as much.

LARRY: Well, you were right to. And I mean it. I hope you know that.

PHIL: I've just had a lot of things on my mind, lately.

LARRY: Like what?

PHIL: (*After a moment*) I've been thinking about making some changes.

LARRY: (*Cautiously*) What kind of changes?

PHIL: I don't know. Just changes.

LARRY: Are you sure that's wise, Phil? I mean, you've had an awful lot of changes imposed on you in recent days. Maybe it's time to let things settle.

PHIL: I've been toying with the idea of pursuing a different line of work.

LARRY: Whaddya mean? Something other than marketing?

PHIL: Yeah.

LARRY: Well, speaking as your friend, Phil. As one who knows you intimately, as it were. I think that's a very bad idea. Dare I say, an entirely shitty idea.

PHIL: Why?

LARRY: Because, A: You were born for this. You have a gift.

PHIL: I'm not Murdock.

LARRY: Nobody's Murdock. Murdock doesn't exist. He's what we pumped him up to be. And two: I don't exactly relish the idea of having to go out on the road with someone new.

PHIL: It's got to happen sooner or later.

LARRY: No, it doesn't. I was always hoping we could end up in a murder-suicide kinda thing.

PHIL: What about Bob?

LARRY: What about him?

PHIL: He's a bright young guy. He's got a way with people.

LARRY: You're suggesting they bring Bob into the shop? Come on, Phil. Get serious.

PHIL: It's been done.

LARRY: You've had far too much to drink, my friend. It's the club soda talking.

PHIL: He's a nice kid. You said so yourself.

LARRY: What do I know.

PHIL: He's got a good head on his shoulders.

LARRY: Let's just drop it. Shall we?

    (*Pause*)

PHIL: (*Distantly*) I've been thinking about a lot of other things, lately, too.

LARRY: Well, look, Phil. If something's bothering you, get it out. It's not good to let things fester. What exactly have you been thinking so much about?

PHIL: Life.

LARRY: Life?

PHIL: And death.

LARRY: (*Exasperated*) Jesus. Not you, too. Why is it all of a sudden everybody's thinking about life and death? Is there something nobody's telling me, that I should know about? Sunspots or something? Is there a plague coming to wipe us from the globe?

PHIL: Strange things happen.

LARRY: No they don't. Not unless they're published first in USA Today. Jesus comes again, he's gotta give 'em two days notice. Time to work up one of those little graphs.

PHIL: I've been thinking about God, lately, too. Wondering.

LARRY: About God?

PHIL: Yeah.

LARRY: What about him?

PHIL: I don't know. Haven't you ever just "wondered" about God?

LARRY: Sure I have. Everybody wonders about God now and then. It's just that some of us don't dwell on it. We give it a place. I believe what I believe.

PHIL: Which is what?

LARRY: How should I know.

PHIL: When I was a little kid, I had a dream about God. I dreamt I found him hiding in a closet in the middle of a burned-out city. There was a city that had been destroyed by a fire or some kind of explosion. And right in the middle of it was this one coat closet— standing there, all by itself. I walked up to it and opened the door. And there inside was God. Hiding. I remember he had this big lion's head. But I knew it wasn't a lion. It was God. And he was afraid. So I offered him my hand and drew him out of the closet. And I said, "Don't be afraid, God. I'm on your side." Then we stood there—just the two of us. Hand in hand, looking out over the destruction. It was just after sunset; I don't know why. But all my life I've been haunted by the feeling I've got some kind of mission here on Earth.

LARRY: A mission?

PHIL: Yeah.

LARRY: What kind of mission?

PHIL: I have no idea.

LARRY: I'll tell you your mission. Your mission, my friend, is the same as mine. To act as a liaison between parties. We are the ambassadors of the new order.

PHIL: Things like that don't bother you, huh.

LARRY: Whaddya mean? Dreams?

PHIL: Questions of God.

LARRY: We're all gonna find out sooner or later, Phil. And in the meantime, my wondering isn't gonna change anything. So why lose sleep. I get precious little as it is.

PHIL: What if something depends on it?

LARRY: On what I believe about God?

PHIL: Yeah.

LARRY: (*Sincerely*) Well, then I made my choices the best I knew how, and I'll just have to live with the consequences.

PHIL: But still, you wonder. Don't you.

LARRY: I'm human, Phil.

PHIL: I know.

LARRY: We're all very tired, Phil. It's the nature of the business.

PHIL: I am aware of that.

LARRY: You've just been under a lot of stress, lately.

PHIL: Is that what it is?

LARRY: You're damn right. What you need is a vacation.

PHIL: I just had a vacation.

LARRY: Well, then you need another one. Or maybe just a good hot date.

PHIL: Yeah?

LARRY: You need what's-her-name. That blonde.

PHIL: Susan?

LARRY: Exactly. Susan. Here's what you do. Soon as we get back to Chicago, you call 'em up at work. Say, "I'd really like to come in this afternoon, but frankly I'm having a hard time giving a fuck as to whether I live or die. So send my checks to the house for a coupla weeks, and I'll see you guys later." Then you call up...

PHIL: Susan.

LARRY: Susan. That's right. You call her up. Tell her you've made reservations up in the Dells. Buy yourself a gross or two of condoms. Take her up there, and go at it like hamsters in heat. Forget about work. Forget about everything. Just get your ashes hauled.

    (*Pause*)

PHIL: (*Distantly*) Do you love me, Larry?

LARRY: (*Taken aback*) Do I love you?

PHIL: Yeah.

LARRY: Well... that depends on what you mean, Phil. If you mean, am I willing to bear your children, then no, I don't love you. I mean, sure, I probably love you. Just not that much. Why do you ask?

PHIL: It's just a question.

LARRY: Do I love you? Sure. Yeah. How could I not? You've got good hygiene. You're a snappy dresser. You don't talk with your mouth full. What's not to love about that?

PHIL: (*Without anger*) Forget it.

LARRY: (*Genuinely*) Do I love you, huh. I don't know. That's a tough question. What brought that to mind?

PHIL: I was thinking about one of the Bible verses I learned as a kid. It was Jesus saying, "Greater love has no man than this; that he lays down his life for his friends."

LARRY: You're asking me would I die for you?

PHIL: I guess so.

LARRY: Well, geez, Phil. That's pushing things kinda far, dontcha think? I mean, what kinda nonsensical question is that? What situation could possibly arise that I would be called on to die for you?

PHIL: Beats me.

LARRY: I mean,… what. You want me to take a flying leap off the balcony? No. I wouldn't do it.

PHIL: I wouldn't ask you to.

LARRY: Even if you did. I'd say, "Phil, my friend. We have enjoyed a long and happy relationship these past I-don't-know-how-many years. But in answer to your request. No. Fuck you. I'm not gonna jump off the balcony." And I would dismiss myself. No hard feelings.

PHIL: As well you should.

LARRY: But do I love you? That's tough. (*Mostly to himself*) I'm not sure who I love. There's a lot of people I like. I think I'm easy to get to know. But love. That's a whole different matter.

PHIL: Don't worry about it.

LARRY: Yeah.

> (*Pause*)

PHIL: What time is it.

LARRY: Who knows.

> (LARRY *gets up to freshen his drink.* PHIL *glances inadvertently at the television.*)

PHIL: I was watching the sign-off on this Channel 20 last night. They were showing scenes of Nature. Waterfalls and whatnot. They showed this one shot of mountain goats being chased by a helicopter. It was really amazing. They'd be moving one direction, then, all of a sudden. Bam! They're moving another. Just Bam! Bam! Like that. Dancing across these little crags. No time at all to think about what they're doing. But you see them at other times. At the zoo. They stumble around. It's like they have no idea where they're going unless they move. Their lives are based on impulse.

LARRY: (*Pointedly*) Susan, Phil. Don't dismiss the idea outright.

PHIL: (*Blankly*) I won't.

> (BOB *enters, a little disappointed to discover that* LARRY *is still present at this late hour.*)

LARRY: There he is.

PHIL: I told you.

LARRY: How'd it go?

BOB: Okay.

LARRY: Did you find him?

BOB: Yeah. I found him.

LARRY: And?

BOB: (*Hesitantly*) And... we talked.

LARRY: And?

BOB: And nothing. We just talked.

LARRY: What did you talk about, Bob?

> (*Beat*)

LARRY: Bob? What did you talk about.

BOB: A lot of different things.

LARRY: Like what, Bob. Give us a for instance. Did you give him our cards?

BOB: I didn't get a chance.

LARRY: You didn't—

BOB: I'm sorry.

LARRY: Did you mention that Phil and I were anxious to meet with him? To discuss what we have to offer?

BOB: No.

LARRY: Then what did you talk about, Bob?

> (*Pause.* BOB *collects his resolve.*)

BOB: We talked about Christ.

LARRY: You talked about...

BOB: Jesus.

> (*Beat*)

LARRY: (*With forced calm*) What, exactly, did you say about Jesus, Bob? Did you mention, perhaps, what line of industrial lubricants Jesus would've endorsed?

PHIL: Larry—

> (LARRY waves PHIL off.)

LARRY: What did you say to him, Bob.

BOB: We discussed things.

LARRY: Concerning Jesus.

BOB: Concerning... a lot of things.

LARRY: In relation to...

BOB: Jesus.

LARRY: Yes. Jesus. I see. (*After a moment*) So you didn't talk about lubricants at all, I take it.

BOB: The nature of the conversation steered itself away from that.

LARRY: The "nature" did. All by itself.

BOB: Yes.

LARRY: The things that were said just sorta took on a life of their own, and before you knew it, there you were, talking about God. Or Jesus. Excuse me.

BOB: We were just having a conversation. It was two people talking.

LARRY: You did not suggest or direct it in any way, then.

BOB: No. We just... it was talking.

LARRY: (*Evenly, after a moment*) Bob. I'm about to say something. Something I don't say to very many people, unless I really and truly mean it. Because, to me, it's like telling someone to go to hell. That's what it means to me.

BOB: What is it?

LARRY: It's that I don't believe you, Bob.

BOB: You don't—?

LARRY: Believe you. Yes. I have a hard time convincing myself that what you just said is true.

BOB: It is true.

LARRY: Perhaps. But I'm having a hard time with it. You understand.

PHIL: Larry, come on—

LARRY: (*Erupting*) Leave me alone, Phil! I'm trying to deal with things here. Okay? So just, please. Don't interrupt.

BOB: It's all right.

LARRY: (*Forced calm, bordering on sweetness*) There. You see? It's all right. (*To* BOB, *after a moment*) Bob. I want to ask you a question. And I want a very straightforward answer. Will you give me that?

BOB: Of course.

LARRY: Don't say "of course." A truly straightforward answer is not that easy to come by. It takes some doing. Just say, "yes," if that's what you mean.

BOB: Yes.

LARRY: What I want to know, Bob, is this. Who suggested. Who mentioned, if you will. The subject of Jesus. Who brought it up. Honestly.

(BOB *looks to* PHIL *for a moment. Pause*)

BOB: (*Quietly*) I did.

LARRY: You.

BOB: Yes.

LARRY: Mentioned Jesus. First. Broached the subject, as it were.

BOB: Yes.

LARRY: Okay, Bob. I appreciate your honesty. You could've lied to me, but you didn't, and I appreciate that. I would've known, but that's beside the point. The point is, you didn't. Now. What I would also like to know. In that same vein. Frankly. Is. Why?

BOB: Why did I bring it up?

LARRY: Yes, Bob. What compelled you to bring up the subject of Jesus. Out of the blue.

BOB: It wasn't out of the blue. It's part of what we were discussing here at the bar.

LARRY: Okay, Bob. Granted. Here. There. It doesn't matter. What I need to know is. *Why*?

BOB: Because it's very important to me that people hear about Jesus.

LARRY: You mean that he died for their sins?

BOB: Yes.

LARRY: That he will accept them into heaven if they follow his teachings?

BOB: If they believe and are baptized. Yes.

LARRY: Okay. Let me restate my question, then, Bob. My question is. Knowing what you now know about the nature of our mission here. What you knew BEFORE you left to go find him. Understanding that it was quite important—I'm wanting to say, *essential*—to our being here that we meet and talk with Mr. Fuller concerning the lubricant situation. Why did you choose, instead, to speak to him about Jesus. That's what I want to know.

BOB: Because I think it's more important.

LARRY: More important. Than our situation. You think that.

BOB: Yes. The "situation" does not mean as much to me as the fate of the man's soul.

LARRY: Is that right.

BOB: Yes.

LARRY: You truly feel that way.

BOB: I truly feel that way.

LARRY: Even though we're at a convention—where it is more customary to talk about business. Etcetera.

BOB: The Apostle Paul said to be ready "in season and out of season—"

LARRY: (*A cry to the heavens*) DON'T QUOTE SCRIPTURE TO ME, BOB! (*Evenly again, after a moment*) Would you? Please? I'm trying to carry on a conversation with you, here. Do not—I repeat, DO NOT—interject quotes from the word of God to me. Leave God out of this, okay? I don't need that. What I'm looking for is something else entirely.

BOB: I don't see how we can have a conversation like this, if I'm not allowed to bring up the subject of God.

LARRY: God is not relevant to this issue, Bob. We are talking about something a great deal bigger than God, here, if I may.

BOB: Bigger than God?

LARRY: Bigger than your belief in God. Let me state it that way so as not to offend. We're talking about something larger.

BOB: For me, there is nothing larger.

LARRY: (*Forcefully*) AT ISSUE here, Bob. Is not your belief in God. Or your desire to spread that belief. At issue is what we're here for. The purpose of our being.

BOB: Which is what?

LARRY: We're here to sell lubricants, Bob. Industrial lubricants. We're not here to save souls.

BOB: We're not here to chase women, either, but that doesn't seem to stop you.

LARRY: Hey! Don't you dare throw that back in my face! Understand me? There is nothing wrong with admiring the scenery while you're doing business. AS LONG AS you're doing BUSINESS. It's when you stop DOING BUSINESS that it becomes a sin. And for your information, SON. I do not chase women. Get me? Fifteen years in this business. Fifteen years here doing exactly this. Never—not once—have I cheated on my wife. I have looked at women. Admired them, yes. Desired in my heart to see a couple of 'em naked. But that's as far as it ever goes.

BOB: If you look at a woman with lust, it's the same as committing adultery.

LARRY: No, goddammit! It is not! There's one helluva difference, Bob—lemme tell ya. Looking at a woman. Desiring her. Wanting to find yourself in bed next to her. Inside her, if I may be so graphic. Walking AWAY from that, for the sake of the rest of your life that you don't wanna destroy. The people you don't want to hurt. Saying to yourself, "I have a wife. We get along. It is not worth it to me to do damage to that for the sake of what I'm feeling at this moment." There is nothing incorrect about that.

BOB: That's not what Jesus said.

LARRY: Well, then goddammit, Bob! Jesus was wrong! If he said that. If that's what he really meant. Then I take exception with Jesus, as presumptuous as that sounds. There is nothing wrong with having an adult desire, if you've got the presence of mind to control yourself.

BOB: I'm just telling you what he said.

LARRY: How do you know what Jesus said, Bob. Someone told you. You read it in a book. Someone else heard it. It was handed down. That's all you know. Period. You don't know that it's true, just as I don't know that it's not true. Because neither of us was there.

BOB: If you look at the evidence—

LARRY: (*Vehemently*) I am not gonna let you tangle me up in a conversation about religion, here. Understand? Religion is beside the point.

BOB: Then what is the point!

LARRY: The point is. That by talking to Mr. Fuller about Jesus instead of handing him our business cards. By doing what you wanted instead of what you're here for—I.E., to represent your employer. You, Bob, betrayed a trust. You said to this company, in effect, "You guys can go fuck yourselves. I don't care that you're paying my way; I'm going to go and do this other thing that doesn't concern you. I'm going to commit adultery, if you will, against the company." Do you follow me? Because what you did, Bob, was a betrayal. And I don't care that you thought you were doing something noble. Men cheat on their wives all the time because they feel they're answering some higher call. There's no difference. Out here. On the road. You are married to the company. She is paying your way. And to betray her like that is to go whoring. To look at a man—to say to yourself, "Gee. I wish I could talk to him about Jesus." To mention it during a break in the action. While you're waiting for a table at dinner. In the john. Fine. To say, "Here's my card. Call me. We'll talk." Also fine. Nothing wrong with that. I like the roundness of a woman's ass, if she takes care of herself, and you look for hurting souls. That's fine for both of us as long as we don't let it get in the way of business. BUSINESS, Bob, is why we're here! Do you understand that?

BOB: Yes! I understand! I just don't see the crime in speaking to another human being as another human being! I don't see why we have to become these *functions* you keep talking about! I mean, where is the line drawn? When do we stop being human? When we park the car at the airport? When we sign our names to the hotel register? Where is it written that we can't relate to one another as *people*?

LARRY: It's not "written" anywhere—

BOB: I didn't mention work or lubricants or anything like that, because it would have diluted the importance of what I was trying to say. He would've thought I was using the subject of religion to cozy up to him and get him to sign some contract. I did not want him to think I was insincere.

LARRY: You were insincere, Bob. In a much bigger sense—

BOB: I mean, if we're nothing but functions here, why don't they just send robots!

LARRY: They don't send robots, Bob, for the simple reason that nobody's invented one yet. The day comes when they can build a robot to do what we do—*and make it work*—then that's exactly what they'll do. Precisely. Until that day, they send us. They say, "Go spend a coupla days in Wichita. Walk around. Meet some people. Don't worry about your room and board. We'll take care of that. Just go." And we, Bob. For a couple of days here in Wichita. We lose our identities and become the hands of the company—shaking all the other hands before us. What *you* did was to sever that bond. It would be like the hand pulling away from the arm and saying, "Look. I've got an interest of my own to pursue which doesn't involve you. I'll be back when I'm through." Would it do that? No. Why? Because without the rest of the body, it has no purpose for being. That's what I'm trying to get you to see.

BOB: (*Rigidly*) I still go back to what the Apostle Paul said.

LARRY: The Apostle Paul was not sent to Wichita to hawk lubricants! Which you were!

BOB: All right, then! I'm sorry! What do you want from me!

PHIL: (*Emphatically, troubled*) Larry. Leave him alone!

LARRY: (*To* PHIL, *desperately*) Will you?! Please?! I'm trying to get something across to him here!

PHIL: With or without the account, WE'LL LIVE.

LARRY: It doesn't matter whether or not we'll live. Can't you see that? It's gone way beyond that now! (*To* BOB) What I'm trying to get you to do, Bob, is take some responsibility, instead of falling back on what somebody long ago may or may not have said!

PHIL: (*Exploding*) GODDAMIT, LARRY! YOU'RE NOT HIS FATHER!

> (*Pause.* LARRY *gazes at* PHIL *as if to say, "What are you doing?"*)

PHIL: You're not.

LARRY: (*Desperately*) Why are you all of a sudden...

> (LARRY *closes his eyes and seems to employ great determination in order to collect himself. Pause.*)

LARRY: You're absolutely right, Phil. I'm not his father.

> (*Beat*)

LARRY: Forgive me, Bob. For behaving as though I were your father. For trying to give you a little something of what I am.

BOB: It's all right.

LARRY: (*Pointedly, to* PHIL) We'll live, I guess.

PHIL: (*Gently*) We will. Live.

LARRY: I believe I just said that. (*After a moment*) Now, if you'll excuse me. I'm suddenly very conscious of the lateness of things. What time do you want to get together in the morning.

PHIL: It doesn't matter.

LARRY: What time.

PHIL: Seven-thirty.

LARRY: Make it eight.

PHIL: Fine. Eight.

LARRY: Fine.

> (LARRY *gathers his suit coat and heads for the door.*)

PHIL: Larry.

> (LARRY *stops at the entrance to the foyer, but does not turn around.*)

PHIL: Goodnight.

LARRY: (*With remorse, after a moment*) Sorry.

> (LARRY *exits.* PHIL *and* BOB *remain still for a time.*)

BOB: I guess I'll be going, too.

PHIL: Not just yet.

> (*Beat*)

PHIL: There's something I want to say to you, Bob. And I want you to listen close, because it's very important.

BOB: What is it?

PHIL: The man I just chased from here.

BOB: You didn't chase—

PHIL: THE MAN WHO LEFT THE ROOM. Moments ago. Is a very good friend of mine. Now. You ask yourself why. Is it because I've know him a long time? There are many people, Bob, I have known for quite a long time. Some of them, I wouldn't let wipe my dog's ass. Others, I could take or leave. They don't matter to me, irrespective of how long I've known them. But Larry matters very much. The reason being, I trust him. I know I can trust him. He's honest.

BOB: Is he honest? Or is he just blunt?

PHIL: He is honest, Bob. He is blunt, as well. That's sometimes a part of being honest. It doesn't prove anything, no. There are people who are blunt without being honest. Larry is not one of those. Larry is an honest man.

>   (*Beat*)

PHIL: You, too, are an honest man, Bob. I believe that. Somewhere deep down inside you is a thing that strives to be honest. The problem is, it has not yet touched the whole of your life. To be honest, Bob. To have honesty means. To have the potential—the *potential*—to see things in a certain light. To attain a frankness, which you can apply or not at your discretion. It does not mean to grab ahold of some standard and wave it around. To impose your vision of right and wrong on everything that crosses your path. No one respects that.

BOB: Jesus—

PHIL: (*Angrily*) Don't you start that shit with me, Bob! I'm being straight with you here! Now, goddammit, you show me the same respect! We're not talking religion. We're talking about what it means to live!

>   (*Pause*)

PHIL: You asked me, before, about character. We were talking about faces, but the question is bigger than that. The question is, do you have any character. And if you want my honest opinion, you do not. For the simple reason that you don't regret anything yet.

BOB: I don't regret anything?

PHIL: That's right. Your life is featureless.

BOB: You're telling me I won't have any character until I do something I'll regret?

PHIL: No, Bob. I'm saying you've done plenty of things to regret, already. You just don't know what they are. It's when you discover them. When you see the folly in something you've done, and you wish you had it to do over; but it's too late for that now, and you know it. So you pick that thing up and carry it with you to remind yourself that life goes on. The world will spin without you. You're not all that important, in the end. Then, Bob, you will attain character. Because honesty will have reached out from inside you and tattooed itself all over your face. Until that day, however, you cannot expect to go beyond a certain point.

> (*Pause*)

BOB: (*Blankly*) May I go now?

PHIL: We're still friends, Bob.

BOB: May I leave? Please?

> (*Beat*)

PHIL: Go ahead.

BOB: Thank you.

> (BOB *turns to go.* HE *stops just before stepping into the foyer.*)

BOB: Phil?

PHIL: Yes, Bob.

BOB: (*Formally, after a moment*) I am grateful for what you did today. Showing me around.

PHIL: You're welcome, Bob.

> (BOB *exits.*)

PHIL: (*Quietly, to himself*) Goodnight.

> (PHIL *goes to the bar and picks up a bottle of club soda. As* HE *unscrews the cap, his eyes alight on a bottle of gin.* HE *picks up the gin and gazes at the label for a moment. His cell phone rings.* HE *answers, inadvertently keeping hold of the gin.*)

PHIL: (*Answering*) Hello?... No, you just missed him... I don't know. Call the front desk...

> (*Pause*)

PHIL: Look. It's been a long day for all of us. Get some sleep.

(PHIL *moves to end the call. Suddenly,* HE *stops dead still.*)

PHIL: What's that?

(*Long pause*)

PHIL: Yeah. (*After a moment*) I love you, too.

(HE *ends the call and sinks down into the couch, staring blankly at the television for a time, cradling the bottle of gin. Lights fade slowly to black. After a moment, the television flickers off.*)

END

Made in the USA
Columbia, SC
25 April 2020